DEDICATIONS

It is a great honor and privilege for me to dedicate this book to the source of my life: God the Father, Son and Holy Spirit. It is because of that trinity that I am able to write and have wonderful Women of God write such a book as, "From the Hearts of First Ladies."

To the bone of my bone and flesh of my flesh, Bishop Gary Hawkins, Sr., I will **always** love you till death do us part. You are my inspiration. It is you who have led the path of excellence for me to follow. Thank you for bringing out the best in me and encouraging me to write this book.

My beautiful daughters: Elaina and Ashley and my handsome sons: Gary, Jr. and Kalen; thank you for your support, love and patience. You never complained during the course of my writing. I am forever grateful to each of you and I am blessed to call you my children.

Finally, I dedicate this book to two of the most precious people on the face of this earth, my mother: Elzina Marie Owens and my mother-in-love, Mary Louise Robertson. You are angels sent from above. Thank you for being prayer intercessors and demonstrating unconditional love.

From the Hearts of First Ladies

THIS BOOK BELONGS TO:

_____

From the Hearts of First Ladies

DEBBIE E. HAWKINS

NILES, ILLINOIS

Copyright © 2005 Debbie E. Hawkins
First Edition

Printed in the United States of America

Published by:
Mall Publishing Company
5731 West Howard Street
Niles, Illinois 60714
877.203.2453

Book Cover Design by Quiana Rosemond

Book Design by Marlon B. Villadiego

All rights reserved. No part of this book may be reproduced or transmitted in any form or by any means, graphic, electronic, or mechanical, including photocopying, recording, taping, or by any information storage or retrieval system, without the permission in writing from the publisher.

Unless otherwise noted, all scripture quotations are from the King James Version (KJV) of the Holy Bible.

ISBN 0-9774291-4-8

For licensing / copyright information, for additional copies or for use in specialized settings contact:

Debbie Hawkins Ministries
P.O. Box 871172
Stone Mountain, Georgia 30087
Phone: 770.498.5850   Fax: 770.498.1566
Email: vof@voicesfaith.org   Website: www.voicesfaith.org

CONTENTS

Dedications I

Table of Contents VII

Acknowledgements IX

Foreword XIII

Introduction XV

Chapter One:
From the Heart of Elder Debbie E. Hawkins 1

Chapter Two:
From the Heart of Dr. Bridget Hilliard 13

Chapter Three:
From the Heart of Dr. Dee Dee Freeman 23

Chapter Four:
From the Heart of Dr. Jewel Tankard 31

Chapter Five:
From the Heart of Pastor Barbara Easley 53

Chapter Six:
From the Heart of Dr. Angela Manning 67

Chapter Seven:
From the Heart of Elder Anita Jackson 75

Chapter Eight:
From the Heart of Evangelist Carol Caldwell 83

Chapter Nine:
From the Heart of Dr. Tracy Pickett 91

Conclusion 105

About the Author 107

ACKNOWLEDGEMENTS

Dear God, I love you. Thank you for giving your only son, Jesus to save my life. It is because of His blood that this book is written. Thank you for allowing me to serve you as a First Lady and to experience and share your love.

To the love of my earthly life, you are the key that unlocks the door to my heart. It has been said that actions speak louder than words. That's a true statement. You have not only expressed with words your love for me but you consistently demonstrated what a loving husband, friend and Pastor, is. Bishop Gary Hawkins, Sr., you are everything I want and need in a companion. Thank you for pushing me to reach for the skies.

To my daughters, Elaina and Ashley, words cannot express my love for the both of you. You have made me so proud to be your mother. Thank you for all you do and the things you do that go unnoticed. You have given me what I wanted and expected from daughters. You are my angels! Thank you for being willing vessels who wants to be used by God.

To my sons, Gary Jr. and Kalen, I prayed and asked God to give me two Godly sons and He answered my prayers when He gave me you. Thank you for being respectable gentlemen who at such a young age love and trust God. Thank you for keeping me in shape as I run to keep up with the both of you. You are my pride and joy!

To my mom, my morning coffee, Elzina Marie Owens, there is no love like your love. Thank you for your compassion, strength and encouragement. Thank you for the many hours you travail in prayer for me. I know God hears and honors your prayers. I will always love you!

To my mother-in-love, Mary Louise Robertson, you are such a kind, meek, and gentle woman. I am privileged to be your daughter-in-love. Thank you for teaching me the meaning of humbleness, a trait you wear so well. I love you!

Special recognition must go to an awesome woman of God, my assistant, Valerie Murkison. You are a true trooper! God has gifted you with many talents. Not everyone can juggle multiple tasks at the same time, but you can. Thank you for making my load liter, thank you for the many sacrifices you make, and thank you for working tirelessly to serve God. You are an asset to the body of Christ. Thank you for helping build God's kingdom on this earth. I love you!

To Quiana Rosemond, Taronda Durante, Cynthia Ward, Mona Brawley and Valerie Morgan, God bless you all. I am forever grateful to you for assisting me with the graphics design and editing of this book. Your contributions are what made this book complete. I pray God continues to bestow many blessings upon each of you. I love you all!

To James Murkison and Tyrone Lane, you are men after God's own heart. Thank you for your servant

mentality. I am so appreciative of all you do. I pray God's anointing continue to be upon your life. I love you both.

To my brothers, Earl and Jasper Leaven, thank you for having my back. You have always supported me and your love is unquestionable. I pray that God will prosper you in all your endeavors. My sister-n-love, Paula Leaven, and my good friend, Therese Nobles, I didn't forget you, thank you for being the sisters I never had. I love all of you, stay focus on God.

To my brother and sister-in-love, Aaron and Mia Hawkins, You are examples of true servants for God. Thank you for standing for righteousness.

To my cousins, Bessie Dudley, Ruthie Dudley and Thelma Jean Taylor, I will forever be grateful to you for protecting and watching over me when I could have gone astray. I love you!

To Dorothy Charles, the aunt I never had. Thank you for teaching me how to be a lady and speaking wisdom in my life. I love you.

In memory of my deceased uncle, Joseph Dudley, I am reminded of the positive reinforcement he always spoke in my life. I am thankful for him speaking into existence, my prosperity.

FROM THE HEARTS OF FIRST LADIES

To John, Reginald, Denita, Wayne, Aldreamer, Mary, Warren, Victorina, Chris, Therese, Gladys, Gail, and Ann, thank you for accepting me into the family. May God overflow you with His blessings.

To the rest of my nieces, nephews, cousins and friends, who are too many to name, I love you sincerely and pray the favor of God on your life.

To the pastoral staff: Althea Brooks, Lorraine Dykes, Barbara Jones, Angia Levels, Lakisha Chatman, Kathleen Dunnings, Neva Romaine, David Ferebee, Mark Berry, Zenda Duren, Debra Adams, Carla Alexander and Laura Walker. You are the best. I love you!

Special thanks to Greg and Betty Levette, Yvette Miller, Mark and Yolette Duncan, Vervela Harris, Bernie Stockard, Gerrie Claxton, Dawn Johnson, Mattie Adams, Genice Johnson and all of the Women with Voices Planning and Prepartion team. You all are the best. Thank you for all you do and your tireless efforts to please God. I love you!

My Voices of Faith Family, I love you and "It's A Family Affair," Thank You for Coming to See Why!

Finally, to all women, be encouraged and remember God has a purpose for each of us. Know with conviction, that you are special and that you have power. You may not be able to move the mountains in your life, but you do have the strength to climb the mountains and speak to the mountains. You are Victorious and I love you!

FOREWORD

Thank God for the vision placed upon First Lady, Elder Debbie Hawkins for sharing her life experiences while also, gathering the experiences of pastors' wives and passing them on as a blessing to all of us. This book offers women wisdom, hope and encouragement as they walk hand-in-hand with their husbands in ministry. Each experience shared by the wives offers unparalleled insight and perspective allowing the reader to embrace her uniqueness in being a "pastor's wife." I applaud the women for their transparency and willingness to share not only their victories but also their failures to explain how they allowed God to mold them in the process. In a world where others are looking to us to always have it together, it's refreshing to know that we are ALL on the Potter's wheel being made for His glory. Where was this book when I first became a pastor's wife?!!

Elder Vanessa G. Long,
First Lady, New Birth Missionary Baptist Church, Lithonia, Georgia

INTRODUCTION

Some of the most beautiful and graceful creatures on earth are "butterflies." It is hard to believe that they were once a wormlike creature called a "caterpillar" that as it grew began to break out of its shell. In many ways First Ladies of our churches are like butterflies—delicate at first, but steadily growing stronger and stronger with each cycle of the ministry. As First Ladies mature spiritually, they exit the cocoon/pupa stage, the third phase of a Butterfly's life cycle.

This test prepares us for the journey God has planned to help us soar higher and higher. God knows when He created His First Ladies there would be times when we flutter but we must remain on course to help build God's kingdom on earth.

In this book, nine beautiful butterflies share their testimonies of fulfilling the call of ministry as ordained by God. Each of these women have incredible, thought-provoking stories that will certainly encourage and lift your spirit to conqueror all of life's obstacles.

I pray through the reading of this book that your life will no longer be the same. I can see you changing before my very eyes into the butterfly God intended you to be!

I love you. Enjoy the book.

CHAPTER ONE

FROM THE HEART OF

Elder Debbie E. Hawkins

VOICES OF FAITH MINISTRIES
STONE MOUNTAIN AND CONYERS, GEORGIA

The Heart of a First Lady

Many people have become addicted to so many things such as drugs, alcohol, sex, money, fame, music, television, and the list goes on and on. If I had to say I was addicted to anything, I would say that I am addicted to being a First Lady. You may be asking, "Well, what does that mean?" It means that I am a lady who understands the law of order. I understand that I must **First,** accept Jesus Christ as Lord and Savior. I must **First** have God as the head of my life. I must **First** be obedient and be governed around Godly principles. I must be the **First** lady in the life of my husband, the **First** lady in the life of my children and the **First** lady to represent the church my husband and I have been called to pastor.

First Ladies have been called by God. That is something that so many fail to recognize or understand. Why? Because tradition has tried to paralyze First Ladies into thinking that their job was simply to sit on the front row of the church, wear a big hat, nod their heads, and look pretty. They were not encouraged or taught to exercise their other God-given abilities in the church (*which are discussed in my book entitled, "What Every First Lady Should Know"*). Although, some were able to sing in the choir or play the piano, that is not the extent of the purpose of a First Lady. God called First Ladies when He called their husbands to be a Pastor. God not only placed a calling on our lives before the earth was formed, but He went further when He chose us. The Bible says, "many are called, but few are chosen" (**Matthew 22:14)**. First Ladies are one of the few people chosen to help meet the needs of our husbands in ministry and we should be proud to have such an honorable blessing from God.

In the early days of our ministry, I was that woman who did not understand that I was called to be a First Lady. I did not understand the pain, trials and tribulations I endured, were not for me, but for all those who read this chapter. They were so that I could share with you as a First Lady. I am commissioned to let you know that we are going to experience the peaks and the valleys, but if we trust God in every area of our lives, He will see us through. I learned that if God is for me, it did not matter who was against me. I learned that I am the head and not the tail; I am above and not beneath; I truly can do all things through Christ who strengthens me. I am not saying I have mastered being a First Lady, but I am saying when I speak to myself and say to First Lady Debbie Hawkins, that I am more than a conqueror; I remind myself, that God's Word says, *"I am more than a conqueror,"* which means the situation I am in, I can conqueror it and so much more **(Romans 8: 37)**.

God has taught me that no matter what I may face, it is He whom I serve and He has already given me everything I need to be a First Lady. By serving Him and putting Him **First** in my life, He gives me revelation knowledge of His word to show me how to live a successful and fulfilling life. He teaches me that besides Him, no other person should come before my husband and that I must reverence him, submit to him, love him, and help meet all of his needs. By being a lady who puts God **First,** I can operate in God's Word and in the law of order on earth. Through God's Word, I am taught that I must be the **First** lady in the lives of my children. Next to my husband, I am to nurture my children, teach them right from wrong, and be mommy to them by providing for their needs and wants. We are to also be the **First** to represent Christ's characteristics in our churches. Christ was loving, trusting, compassionate, and had all the Fruit of the Spirit traits. As First Ladies that is exactly how we are to represent Him.

First Ladies were chosen to be women of strength and power, love and compassion. We represent God. Jesus endured good and bad encounters so that we would be able to look to Him as an example in life. We as First Ladies are going to have that same type of experience, if we haven't already; therefore, we are to mirror Christ as an example so that we may be an example for others. Our life on this earth is to represent Christ. Christ was a blessing to us and we are to be a blessing to others.

There is no other position on the face of this earth that I would rather have, than the position of a First

Lady. It is a position that only God can hire you for and it is one of high status that I don't mind working for. I appreciate God and I thank Him for not being a respecter of a person. He did not choose us for the position He gave us based on our education, background, looks, talents, or who we know. He doesn't even take in consideration the things we've done in the past that we shouldn't have done, the places we've gone that we shouldn't have gone, the people we hung out with that we shouldn't have hung out with or the thoughts that have traveled through our minds that were ungodly. Every woman serving in this position as a First Lady has been pre-ordained before the world was ever created.

I don't claim to have all the solutions to the many things encountered in ministry, but you can peep through the window of my testimony (as I served along side of my husband) and see the magnificent hand of God at work. Let's take a look from where it all began:

I have been in church all of my life which is 44 years; but, I have only been in ministry for a little over 11 years. I must say that in those 11 years I have learned and grown in many ways. On the other hand, I spent 28 years in church, coming and going as I pleased, with no strings attached. Five years later, some wonderful and glorious things happened to me that would change my life forever, for the best. I received Christ as my Lord and Savior; I learned how to tithe; and, my husband found me: not broken, but mended; not begging, but giving, and not homely, but intriguing.

My husband and I met in the month of November. In my mind it was love at first site, but in actuality it was God working at His best. We were married in May of the next year. The following year, I was introduced to the world of ministry from a whole new spectrum. Little did I know this was the beginning of my life never being the same again. My husband and I were now leaders who were opening God's doors to teach others how to come to Christ. We started by holding Bible Study sessions at a Recreation Center on Tuesday evenings. Six months later, we gave birthed to Voices of Faith Baptist Church, now known as Voices of Faith Ministries. We moved from the Recreation Center to a nearby church in Decatur, Georgia that allowed us to have worship service at the 11 am hour because they had worship service at the 8 am hour. For two weeks, God blessed us to have over 80 people in attendance. I was so excited to be the Pastor's wife and have a church building to worship God in. Everyone rejoiced like never before until our joy was interrupted by the Pastor and wife who were letting us use their church. They kicked us out for having more people in attendance than they had. Homeless, though we were, the Recreational Center reinstated us and allowed our church to hold Worship Services there once again.

We had about 20 members, but we worshipped with joy and my husband preached like the place was filled to capacity. Every Sunday we had to exercise our faith and see through the eyes of God and not the eyes of man. My brother-in-love, Aaron Hawkins is a hard worker and leads by example, as does his wife, Mia Hawkins. I remember, one Sunday morning, Aaron got to the recreation center early to help with the set-up. He and my husband were setting out the equipment and putting down chairs. They must have placed over a hundred chairs in the area we used for worship service. They did this every Sunday, but on this particular day Aaron finally had to ask the question, "Why are we setting all these chairs down when every Sunday we only have about 20 people in attendance?" My husband, now known as, Bishop Gary Hawkins, Sr., answered him and said, "These chairs are not for those who are coming today, but for those who are coming tomorrow." I must say, I was wondering the same thing as Aaron, but just didn't ask the question. I got delivered that day from small minded thinking and began to think big.

I had to see the big picture. Was I tired? Yes. Were there times when I wanted to give up? Yes. Did I feel like the load was too heavy? Yes. My job was tremendous because I wore so many hats. I was the greeter, did the welcome, ushered, a choir member and prayer leader. I also helped with the cleaning of the facility, helped with the setup, made phone calls, passed out flyers, knocked on doors to get people to come to our church, be a wife, birthed babies, and be a mommy, cooked, worked a full-time job, cleaned house, be a friend and ministered to the sick and broken-hearted. I did not think I would be able to survive, but every morning I had my "morning coffee" to inspire me. My mother, Elzina Marie Owens is my morning coffee. I talk to her every morning and she always says something to nudge me closer to my destination. Every First Lady needs to have someone to be encouraged by and I am so glad she is not only my mother but also my prayer warrior. She helped me learn that this was the life and job of a First Lady and that God would see me through.

I also learned that while I served in all those areas, I had to have tough skin. I had to let certain things that happened to me roll off my back like water rolls off of a duck's back. What do I mean by that? I learned that no matter how hard I worked in ministry, I had to be strong. When people came up to my husband and me and recognized only him, or introduced him only and eventually would come back as an afterthought and say, "Oh, by the way, that's his wife" I had to remember that it is God who I work to please and everything I do should be done so that He may get glory from it.

One year later, we seized a window of opportunity. This time, a church in Stone Mountain opened their doors to us and allowed us to hold worship services at their church. They warned us that even though the area was growing rapidly, they had been in that location for years and people just did not go to church. They said it would be tougher for us because the time slot they were giving us was 7:45 until 9:30 am. But that didn't matter to us, we just wanted to be in a church edifice. Once again we rejoiced and were excited.

God was speedily moving us up the ladder. Our membership grew from 20 to 200 in less than two years. My husband, who was bi-vocational also worked for Delta Airlines so I was enjoying the benefits of flying whenever I wanted to. Then God spoke to my husband and said it was time for him to be totally devoted to ministry and to work the vision He placed in him outside of a full-time job. He said, "Yes, Lord." I supported him 100% knowing it would be challenging, but that God would provide. When we shared the vision with our 200 member congregation the majority of them did not receive the vision. We were worshipping in someone else's church and did not have our own building. The people said we should focus on building a church before having a full-time pastor. My husband and I stood firm on God's Word and all but thirty people left us and the thirty included children.

When it rains, it pours. The next week as we were preparing for Bible Study, the church where we had been worshipping dropped a bomb on us that was intended to blow us away. They kicked us out with no notice because we had become "too comfortable" in their building. We were also in the midst of celebrating our Pastor and First Lady's anniversary that same week. Many people had been invited including a guest artist and a church out of Nashville, Tennessee. We were homeless, again. However, God always provides a ram in the bush. The doors of Stephenson Middle School were opened to us and we celebrated our anniversary giving God all the glory and honor.

Fifteen children and fifteen adults made up our congregation. Hope kept us alive, faith gave us the strength not to give up and trust in God provided for, all our needs. Through the storms that kept on coming, we pressed forward. We never missed a beat. Hope kept us alive, faith gave us the strength not to give up and trust in God provided for, all our needs. The purging experience we had faced made room for God's vision to be manifested. God's finances had superseded what it was when we had 200 members. We grew from 30 to 75 members in two years and built our first Worship Center. We finally had a place to call home. Hope kept us alive, faith gave us the strength not to give up and trust in God provided for, all our needs.

So here we are, eleven years of Voices of Faith Ministries, "The City of Faith," campus that encompasses: 65 acres of land, a 6,000 square foot Children's Sanctuary, an Activity Center, a Daycare Center, an Academy (K3-5th grade School) with a full sized gym and Chapel, a Family Life Center that includes a Kid-Zone (a center for children), Bookstore, Hair salon, Barber shop, Banquet hall, Aerobic room, Weight room, Men's and Women's sauna's, commercial kitchen, classrooms and a second church location in Conyers, Georgia, which is our most recent project, "Voices of Faith East" (currently held at Conyers Middle School at 9:30 am on Sunday Mornings). Voices of Faith East, 35,000 square foot church edifice is in the process of being built. Its anticipated dedication service will be in the spring of 2006.

Ministry has matured me in so many ways. It forced me to grow up quickly, but at the same time it afforded me the opportunity to experience life in ways I only imagined and dreamed of. If I had to start all over again, I would not change anything I have experienced as a First Lady. The tests and trials have resulted in victory!

Always remember, don't let your past or current situation determine your outcome. Just because things may appear one way, does not mean it has to stay that way. Never despise small beginnings, but be willing to work your way up the ladder. I am forever grateful to God for what He has done, is doing, and going to do in my life.

I love you always!

CHAPTER TWO

FROM THE HEART OF

Dr. Bridget Hilliard

NEW LIGHT CHRISTIAN CENTER CHURCH
HOUSTON, TEXAS

The Heart of a First Lady

Life as a Pastor's Wife (The First Lady) Lessons I have Learned

As I begin to reflect over my life, I am amazed even now after 30 years at the life God has allowed me to experience. I have often said I would not want to be anything else in life but a Pastors' wife and, of course, the wife of Dr. Ira Hilliard. I have had the wonderful privilege of enjoying my life to the fullest over the past twenty-one years. However, the first nine years are a book in itself. I will try to capsulize my journey so that you will know and understand what I mean, about those first nine years.

I married my wonderful husband on October 4, 1975 and the very next day October 5th we were installed as Pastor and First Lady of a small denominational church. I was only nineteen years old and the responsibility of being a first lady was placed upon me. My husband, of course, was twenty-three but still we were young and had no experience of being in the position in which we were placed. We stayed at that church about two years and that was quite an experience in itself. My husband began immediately setting the house in order and came up against much opposition.

The church was basically controlled by one family;

the family of the previous Pastor who had passed away. One of the previous Pastor's daughters was married to a man who owned a beer tavern and I know you are going to be shocked at this next statement. The man was using the church money to sustain his cash flow for the beer tavern. Once my husband realized what was being done, he called a church meeting. Prior to the meeting, the man's wife had been known to have killed several people in the past and she stood on the church step and cocked her gun. After everyone was in, she sat on the back row of the church with her gun in her purse. As my husband began the meeting and called for the vote to replace this man on the board, his wife cleared her throat and no one voted to replace him but me. Lesson learned: *As my husband talked with God about why this happened, God responded to him, "Sheep don't fight for shepherds; shepherds fight for sheep." What an eye opening experience!!*

We later left and started another denominational church in a building that we leased sight unseen. That's right! We leased a building from a man and had not seen the inside of the building. Once we entered the building, we saw a beer tavern that was known in the community as the "pill house". This means in the '70's they sold drugs from that place and the entire community knew it. What did we do? Immediately we began to clean up and use everything we had available to us to make the place look like a house of God. We used a desk and some legs from a chair to make our podium. We cleaned up the chairs that people had sat on to drink beer and other alcoholic drinks and they became our first sanctuary seats. We tore down the front of the building and placed a new look on the building. We took down beer signs and painted walls and within a few days we had transformed the once "pill house" into a beautiful house of God. Here we are about almost thirty years later and that building that we transformed is still a church today. Lesson learned: ***When I make a natural decision to do something in my life and with my life that glorifies God, I trigger the supernatural power of God and grace of God to bring it to pass.***

After that experience, God called us to pastor the church that was notorious for replacing the Pastor every year or year and a half. Prior to going, my husband reminded God of the church's reputation and God still said go. Well, after about two years, the board rose up and wanted to put my husband out. This was the most horrifying experience I had ever gone through in my life. We had to go to court. To make a long story short, we won in court and were able to stay at the church. My husband went to church the next Sunday and preached a message about Jacob and Laban entitled, "You Met Your Match". My husband fired the board that had him arrested; yes arrested. My husband fired the board that took him to court and all those that were opposed to his leadership as well. He then went in his office after church and the Spirit of God rebuked him and said, "They were wrong, but they are my people and you had no right to do them like that" God then told him, "Now, get your stuff and leave". WOW!!!! *Lesson learned: No matter how wrong people are it is not your responsibility to vindicate yourself. God says vengeance is His. He will repay!*

We then obeyed God and left that church and started a new church in a building that was 20x20 and infested with termites. We again had to use what we had and allow God to help us. It was in this place that I would go to my car on Sundays, roll up all the windows and not allow my children to talk to anyone. I had been so hurt by the past experience that I did not want to be hurt by people again. My life was miserable, my marriage began to spiral downhill and at the age of 24 years old I almost had a nervous breakdown. I would not allow myself to develop relationships with others; I built a wall and would not let anyone in my territory for fear of being hurt again. I was extremely irritated with people and my life was miserable.

Prior to my husband establishing the church, he had been filled with the Holy Spirit and began to teach others about his new experience with God. I, of course, was not interested and verbally and blatantly told him of my displeasure with him teaching this to others. My comments were like, "You know we were never taught this in our denominational church". Ira was so committed to this new experience that he began to read books and listen to tapes of faith teachers. He was convinced that faith was a lifestyle to which he must commit. I was not at all convinced initially and did not support his commitment to faith and being filled with the Holy Spirit.

One Sunday after the message and after receiving tithes and offerings, my husband stood up in this small church and declared, "The Spirit of God impressed upon me to give my salary today back to the church." Remember, I was not convinced about this new commitment my husband had to the lifestyle of faith or being filled with the Holy Spirit. I was shocked to say the least and could not believe what he had done. This was the week of my birthday and we had no money in the bank, no savings and no food. To make the situation even more complicated, my husband began to point out people whom we would eat with each night. I had to eat so I went each night very unhappy. I know this experience was the turning point in my life.

Wednesday, of that week God began to show me that all that Ira was saying and doing was divinely ordained. Ira went to the church daily to study and pray. While he was there at the church that Wednesday, a member who had not been at church that Sunday came by the church. The member did not just come by to speak; he came by and said, "Pastor, I just received a settlement from an insurance claim and God spoke to me to come by today and give my tithes and offering." The member had no idea what Ira had done that Sunday but he obeyed the Spirit of God. The member not only brought his tithes and offering but he gave us personally several thousand dollars, a cow that he had prepared at the meat market and groceries to go along with the meat.

Needless to say, I was totally convinced and began to read all the books Ira had read, and listen to tapes. After a series of events on September 2, 1982, I was filled with the Holy Spirit in Los Angeles, California at Crenshaw Christian Center. My life began to change drastically. *Lesson learned: God's power is available if you ask Him and that power will transform you as well as areas of your life that you submit to Him. I learned to daily depend on the Holy Spirit as my comfort, my teacher and my guide. I, by faith, appropriated the grace to release every care, every anxiety, every worry on Him and He perfected all that concerned me. It was at this point in my life that I learned to release my faith for favor with God and man according to Luke 2:52.*

Luke 2:52
v. 52 "And Jesus increased in wisdom and stature, and in favour with God and man."

After being filled with the Holy Spirit in 1982, my life changed immediately. I began to learn how to pray according to the word and will of God according to 1 John 5:14-15. I, also, learned Proverbs 18:21,

"Death and life are in the power of the tongue". I immediately changed what I was saying about my life, the ministry and the people of God. I committed to help Ira in ministry as we built into God's people that understanding their purpose and knowing the power of God was available to help them in every area of life and in turn they gave God praise. For two plus years Ira and I read every book Harrison House publishers had available at the time. We developed the discipline to listen to two hours of the word daily from teachers like Dr. Fred Price and others. That focus and discipline were the foundation we needed for the grand announcement we made the first Sunday in September of 1984.

1 John 5:14-15
v. 14 "And this is the confidence that we have in him, that, if we ask any thing according to his will, he heareth us:"

v. 15 "And if we know that he hear us, whatsoever we ask, we know that we have the petitions that we desired of him"

Proverbs 18:21
v. 21 "Death and life are in the power of the tongue: and they that love it shall eat the fruit thereof."

The first Sunday in September of 1984 my husband stood in our traditional church and declared we would no longer be New Light Missionary Baptist Church but New light Church World Outreach and Worship Centers. We had about three hundred people in service that day for the announcement and the very next Sunday we had only twenty-three members. Ninety two percent of our members left in one day. We were so persuaded in the Word by then that we were not moved by what we saw; we were only moved by what we believed. We believed God would build a church of 18,000 members. God honored our faith and today we are the Pastors and Founders of one of the greatest mega churches in the country.

It would take another book to give details on the lessons learned from 1982 to now, but to get to the point, God worked wonders in our lives and I learned many lessons. God is faithful and He will do exactly what His Word says. I am now living in the overflow. Our church has three locations in the city of Houston, one location in Austin and one location in Beaumont. We continue to grow weekly. We currently have a membership of over 20,000. *Lesson learned: If you are willing and obedient, you shall eat the good of the land. If you obey and serve him, you will spend your days in prosperity and your years in pleasure.*

I would not change any experience that I have gone through; mine has been a life worth living. I would not want to be anything else in life other than a "First Lady".

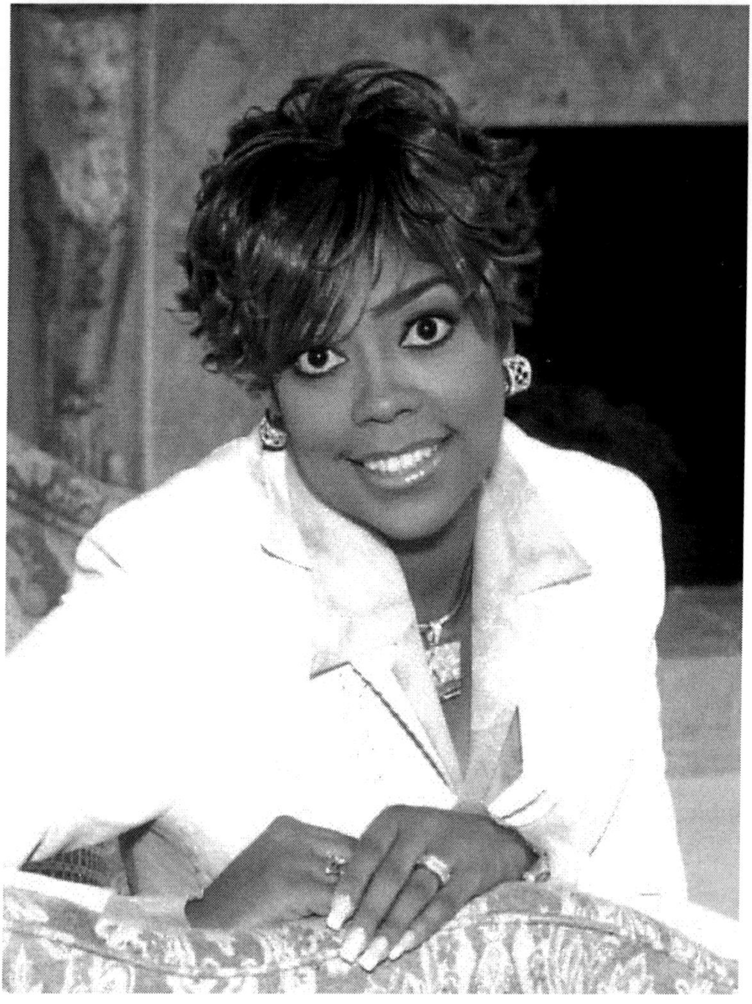

CHAPTER THREE

FROM THE HEART OF
Dr. Dee Dee Freeman

SPIRIT OF FAITH CHRISTIAN CENTER
TEMPLE HILLS, MARYLAND

A Heart of a First Lady

Where should I begin, probably with the cliché of "your life is not your own". My husband, Dr. Michael Freeman (Mike), and I have been married for over 20 years. Mike knew he was called to pastor before we got married. He asked me did I think I could handle the role of being a pastor's wife and of course I said yes. I had no idea of what that meant. I thought that all I had to do was to sit on the second row and wear a big hat. I was sadly mistaken. I had no idea that when God called him, I also would be used in ministry.

The first seven years of our marriage was hell on earth. I just knew that God must have changed His mind. There was no way that He was about to use either of us in ministry. Mike and I were married without any "formal" counseling. All we knew is that we loved each other. So, here we are, young, in love, and unprepared; oblivious to the fact that we were about to go through some of the worst years of our lives. We both had our own view of how marriage should work and unfortunately our separate views caused chaos. As you can probably imagine, this situation went on for days, weeks, months, and eventually years. I was a very independent, strong willed, yet quite emotional woman. This caused me to experience many hours regretting the day I got married.

One day I finally made one of the best decisions of

my life. I divorced myself from my emotional instability and now I have a good marriage. I thank God because at the same time Mike was being challenged to make changes as well. This decision catapulted our lives to the blessed state it is in today.

Now I can say I love being a WIFE first, and then a Mother and then a Pastor's Wife. I cook, clean, take care of my children, do homework and most importantly take care of my MAN. That's right I do "wifely" duties like every other woman should do. Yes, I have days just like you, that I don't want to, but I remember that I have divorced myself from the way I feel and I take care of my business. God has given me the grace to handle everything I need to do. Just like any other wife and mother I must make time to pray and study the Word of God. I must create my quiet and intimate time with the Lord, it doesn't just happen. I have three wonderful children, Brittney (17) she is an ORU Freshman, Joshua (15) he is a sophomore in High School and Brelyn (12) she is in the 7th grade; both Joshua and Brelyn are home schooled.

We have a very successful ministry with two locations: Temple Hills and Brandywine Maryland. Our membership has grown to twelve thousand in twelve years. Our ministry owns a Bible Book Store, a hair salon, a day care center, an upholstery training center, a Family Life Center which houses our computer training center and an accredited Bible Institute.

One of the worst experiences I had as a Pastor's wife was when a female partner in the Ministry called Pastor Mike at our home while I was at my women's meeting. She told him that he knew who she was and that she was the one who could make him happy for real. Pastor Mike tells the young lady that she is sadly mistaken and hangs up the phone and heads for the church where I am holding my meeting. He comes right to the pulpit and says "one of you called my house". You see in all of our new partner classes he tells them if anyone ever comes on to him he would tell. If he did not say anything she would have thought it was a chance or possibility. Now the whole time that this is going on I am tripping on the inside. The girl told him her name but at the time we could not figure out who she was. Time passes by and we are thinking that it is over with.

About two months later after our New Year's Eve service Pastor Mike and I are hugging and greeting the people and I hear "DEE DEE" – I instantly knew that it was Pastor Mike and because of how he said my name I also knew that he needed me right away. So in the midst of all of the people I found him and he grabbed my hand and says, "This is the young lady that called the house". Before I knew it we are in our lounge having a meeting with the young lady, her fiancée, (yes her fiancée), her dad, her sister and our Assistant Pastor. You thought I was going to say before I knew it I stole (or hit) her. I wanted to but I'm saved now. At the conclusion of the meeting, her dad said that he had looked for a church for a long time and he knew that our church was where he was supposed to be and that he was not leaving. He said he didn't know what was wrong with his daughter. The young lady, her fiancée and her sister left the ministry.

Well you would think that would end this story but it doesn't, the young lady and her sister returned to the church. I had to really trust God during this time to keep my heart right (Matthew 5:8). When they returned they acted as if nothing had ever happened. I was thinking that just maybe she would apologize – but still to this day nothing has been said. On top of that there were times when we would have altar calls for different challenges and yes, this young lady would come up in the line for prayer. I wanted to lay my hands on her but not so she would be healed. But at the same time I had to do the Word, even when I did not want to, when I did not feel like it, I had to do the Word. Psalm 119:165 says, "Great peace have they which love thy law, and nothing shall offend them". I could not walk in offense and cut off the blessings of God in my life for a bad choice that someone else made.

Matthew 5:8
v. 8 "Blessed are the pure in heart: for they shall see God."

Even if I were not a Pastor's wife, during that time in my life, I still would have had to take this stand and not allow the actions of others to dictate to me a response outside of the will of God. This experience was a love test for me. I love God's people and I will not allow anything to stop that. You can not judge all women by the actions of one woman.

Today I can boldly and gladly admit that I enjoy being a Pastor's wife. Not because of the so-called glitz and glamour and any other attention that people think the life of a Pastor's wife entails. I love being a Pastor's wife because I love God, and I know that this is my purpose in life. I know who the pastor is so we don't have a lot of the struggles that some are having. I have been called to assist him in ministry and not to take over. I have learned how to honor and submit to my husband, as husband and as Pastor.

From the Heart
of
First Ladies

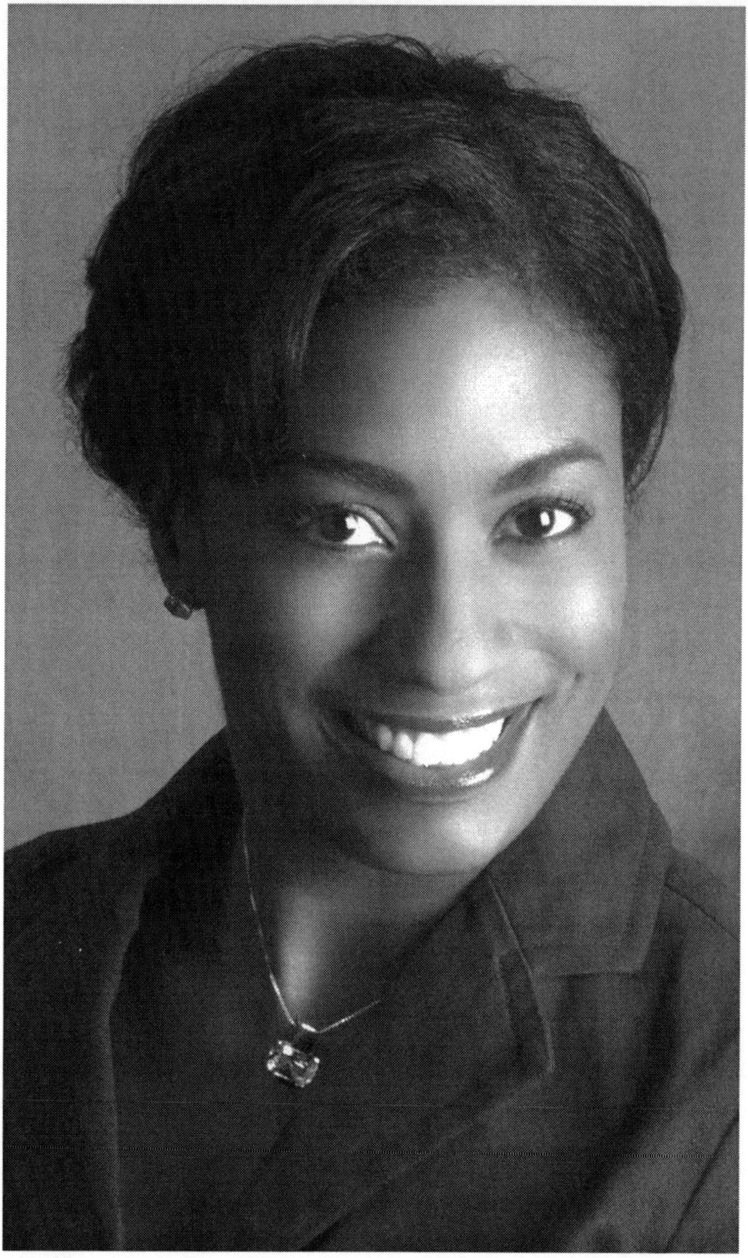

CHAPTER FOUR

FROM THE HEART OF
Dr. Jewel Tankard

DESTINY CENTER
MURFREESBORO, TENNESSEE

The Heart of a First Lady

Mastering the Art of the Leading Lady
We Are All Leading Ladies

Wow! There is so much to share with you regarding the art of being a "Leading Lady". I am a wife, mother, model, motivational speaker, talk show host, business woman and Co-Pastor of Destiny Center to name a few! There is an art to living the God kind of life with grace, joy and continued success. The first thing that I would like to say is that all of us, as women of God, should see ourselves as "Leading Ladies" in every area of life. Whether you are a Pastor's wife, a mother, a sister or a businesswoman, we all possess the power of influence to change and shape our world as leading ladies. God has equipped each of us with the innate ability to develop and bring out the best in those around us.

In our marriages, we are gifted to gently help guide our husbands into greatness and Kingship through honest communication, prayer, love and encouragement. As mothers, with our children, we are each gifted with the ability to and correct, without breaking the unique personalities of our children. As businesswomen, we depend on the Holy Spirit to know how to "think on our feet", make quick and firm decisions while still maintaining grace and beauty. These are just some of the areas that we all can operate as leading ladies in our personal and professional lives.

Jewel's Testimony – Submission: The Key to Every Leading Ladies Success

Allow me to share some of my own background with you. Looking back on my earlier years in my walk with Christ as a single, young, woman, my life was both exciting but also very challenging. Through it all I found that prayer is the key to success. As a young woman of God, I made the decision to give God everything I had, and to pursue Him relentlessly. I was in the prayer room of my church every morning at 6 a.m., and was an intercessor for my spiritual father, Bishop Wayne T. Jackson of Great Faith Ministries in Detroit, MI and his wife. It didn't matter what time of day or night that it was: if I received a call to pray, I would pray. Some nights I would shut myself in the church, fasting and praying and seeking the face of God. I understood very early on that prayer was the secret to understanding the mysteries of the Kingdom of God, and to having great success. As a result, God prospered me in everything I put my hands to do and I account all of those successes to prayer.

Two years after receiving salvation, I married outside the will and timing of God. My Pastor's had instructed me to wait but I thought I "knew it all" and didn't listen to his sound instruction. I was assigned by Bishop Jackson as one of the lead intercessors. With each assignment he gave me, we saw increase through prayer in the ministry, in the area of new members, finance and even divine healing. That same year, Prophetess Juanita Bynum also prophesied to me that I was a powerful intercessor that God would use in mighty exploits. I did have the anointing operating in my life but not the maturity.

An important point here to note is that no matter how anointed you are, *you must always submit and obey the leadership that God has placed you under.* Submission is the key to every leading ladies success. Every woman is only as powerful as her ability to submit to the authority that God has placed her under. I experienced what you might call the "I hear from God too" syndrome, which only led to disobedience and destruction. My marriage was over within two years and I was left alone with a beautiful baby girl and a broken heart. I prayed, fasted, and confessed almost all of the time. I was determined to save the marriage. But when you are not in the perfect will of God (due to your own disobedience), God will not always move the way that you desire. Thankfully, through prayer, *submission and obedience,* the Lord was faithful and restored my life quickly.

I came from a family of entrepreneurs and my parents Earthel and June LaGreen have been in business all of my life. In addition to my modeling and acting opportunities, I had a strong desire to own my own business as well. I partnered up and opened a Nextel franchise in Detroit, MI. It was very successful and grew from nothing to a staff of about 15 in the very first year. I became whole and complete while single and resting in the arms of the Lord.

While busy staying patient and submitted to God's plan for my life – working in ministry, parenting, and being a good financial steward over my businesses, then God sent me the man of my dreams and prayers - Dr. Ben Tankard - my lifetime groom. Ben has been everything to me that I prayed for and so much more. He was the true blessing that the Lord intended for me. He's tall, fine, very wealthy, a man of integrity and a wonderful father. "The Blessing" (which is the anointing of God to prosper in every area of life) was only brought about through submission, obedience and patience with God's plan for my life. I am now using my past experiences (good and bad) as building blocks for our ministry.

The Art & Grace of the Leading Lady

There is definitely an art and a discipline to mastering the role of a leading lady in as it pertains to being a Pastor's wife. I don't personally use the term "1st Lady" because I see myself as not only the first, but also the last and only leading lady of the ministry. I've always felt that "1st Lady" implies, that there may be a second or third to come!

One important part to the art of being a leading lady is lightheartedness! So often, in our culture, women have viewed the role of a Pastor's wife as almost a sentence to hardship and struggle. Some feel that being a Pastor's wife is stressful and lonely. However, I am here to announce that is a lie from the enemy! Being a Pastor's wife is wonderful! Our role is not to be viewed as a weight or burden to bear. We have to remember to keep a light heart and a fresh perspective. Look at your assignment as a Pastor's wife as an opportunity from God.

We have to remember to see the people that we have been blessed to minister to as blessings and not burdens. Don't think of each person that you minister to as a problem, but a possibility! Also understand that you are not solely responsible for any person's destiny but your own. You cannot control what people do in the long run. However, you do have a tremendous influence and ability to impact the lives of your members, your visitor's and viewing audience in a tremendous way; and there will be many that follow your instruction and reap the rewards.

Also, remember to keep your trust in God and not people. For example, if you and your husband are led to give a car away and a year later that person leaves the ministry, it is understandable that you would be disappointed or angry at first. But remember, when you gave the car, it was as unto the Lord and not to the person. Remember, technically, people owe us nothing, though God does use people, our focus must stay on Him and not man. When you do this, you will never be disappointed another day in your life. Be mindful to commit those members that you have been entrusted to oversee to the Lord in prayer and He will help keep your heart and mind free. When your expectation and hope is in God, instead of people, you are never let down. Even if people change, God's word and His promises never change. You can count on that!

The second important point to remember is to have fun, laugh and be adventurous and don't allow the work of the ministry to become a burden to you! Remember that because the Spirit of God appointed you to ministry leadership beside your husband, you are well equipped and anointed to carry it out with grace. Look at each new day as an adventure and rely on the direction of the Holy Spirit when making decisions or giving counsel. Be sure to maintain your regular date night with your husband and plan vacations quarterly. Often, when Dr. Ben and I travel for ministry, we simply plan a few extra days in areas that we like to vacation. We do this often when we travel to Florida, California or out of the country. You can also make special arrangements with the ministries that you are visiting to have your children travel with you. This way, you are keeping your time with your husband and your family first.

If you are invited to minister on your own, take

time before or after the event to enjoy the spa, some shopping or a quiet dinner with your favorite book. You can also invite a good friend or family member to come along to make a "mini-vacation" out of it. Always maintain balance in your life! It isn't all about work, work, work! Integrate your daily responsibilities as well as your prayer and personal time into your "fun time." When you do this, you will find that everyday you have something fun and exciting to look forward to!

When you make the decision to receive the mantle of leadership as a leading lady, with all of its responsibility, the joy and grace of God will overshadow you. Remember, Jesus came to give us life and life more abundantly! Not stress or stress more abundantly! The anointing to accomplish all that He asks you to do will rise up within you. Run to your destiny with excitement and get ready to experience the most exciting walk with God that you can imagine as the leading lady of your ministry! In the following chapter, I want to share some things with you about Prayer, Perspective, Partnership, Mentoring and Passion in Marriage.

Prayer – Our Foundation

The foundation of all life, both natural and supernatural, is prayer. Whatever your life is manifesting right now is a result of prayer, or the lack thereof. I learned this lesson very early in my walk with God.

Before you can ever enter into your purpose and the destiny that God has for you, it is necessary that you establish a solid foundation of consistency in prayer. This is what creates depth and Godly character in you, and saturates you in the anointing of the leading lady. Prayer gives form to and gives birth to all things. Prayer does the hidden work of the inner man, the preparation for purpose that causes you to be propelled into the forefront to take your place as the leading lady. Prayer places the mark of God upon you and the distinction of God's uniqueness to fulfill the role of a leading lady.

As a Pastor's wife, I understand that consistent, frequent times of prayer have been pivotal to the success of my husband and our church. Prayer is the fuel that keeps us over, not under all of the responsibilities and situations that pastors encounter. It keeps us in the flow of success after success, and is the great regulator of our attitudes and emotions. Prayer is not just a traditional habit, but also our lifeline, and the air that we breathe. We are now seeing the fruit of our constant prayer, as pastors and as a congregation.

Prayer will protect you, propel you and prosper you. In conjunction with the Word of God, it will carry you as far, wide and deep as you care to go in God and in life. As a leading lady, mastering prayer will make the difference between success and failure in you, your husband and your church. Therefore, at Destiny Center, in addition to our personal prayer time, we have established a corporate intercessory prayer team and intercessors that pray for us around the clock. Remember, woman of God: Every failure is a prayer failure! When you devote time in prayer, you will walk in victory and success.

Perspective

It is essential that the leading lady have GOD'S perspective, and not the perspective of the people. Your perspective dictates what you say, so be mindful of what is in your heart. Daily identify where you are, and be honest with God about anything that your harbor in your heart that doesn't line up with the Word. Remember God knows anyway, so tell Him, so He can help you.

Referring back to prayer, when you are rooted and grounded in prayer, and in the Word of God, you possess the calm security of knowing who created you, and what your purpose is in Him. God's perspective supercedes the thoughts and attitudes of man. Be very mindful not to allow yourself to build up a negative perspective of people. After counseling hundred and thousands of families through serious and sometime tragic situations, if you aren't careful, you will become callous. I have seen many Pastors' wives begin to build up a wall when it comes to their perspective of people because they don't want to be hurt or disappointed. But remember to keep the Lord's perspective. You should declare and believe that people have good thoughts toward you, your family and your ministry! Make a decision to believe the very best about people because whatever you think on, you will eventually have. So be sure to keep a balanced and fresh perspective. Think on what is good and you will possess it.

You should also schedule time to yourself to have one day of complete rest and relaxation! Even God Himself rested one day of the week! This will allow you to be well rested and ready to interact with thousands or even millions of people each year, because you have given yourself personal time to rest. I commit to making Monday's my "do nothing day". I sleep in for as long as I need to until my body says "wake up". I take extra time to pray and meditate, I work out or whatever I want to do. Doing this, allows me to look forward to ministering and interacting with members and those who reach out to us daily. Keep in mind, you will have to fight for these "off days", but make regular time at all cost.

Know that your perspective dictates your attitude, emotions, circumstances, and your destiny. It is so important that I am able to honestly relay a good perspective to our congregation and to those I mentor of the blessing of being a Pastor's wife. How will people be drawn to serving in the Kingdom and to Pastoring if I have a negative perspective and constantly complaining? Continue to spend time with God in prayer and honestly talk to Him about your life, your dreams and your concerns and He will allow His love to shine from the inside out.

In addition, if you are a "people person" like I am, be sure not to allow tradition to dictate that you should be unapproachable. Be with the people as much or as little as you desire. Be yourself! God gave your personality to you - you have your own unique anointing. Be who God has called you to be and you will have great success! Decide today to keep a good attitude, to let go of any past hurts and to think and expect the best from others and from life!

One of my favorite meditation scriptures is James 1:5, *"If any of you lack wisdom, let him ask of God, that giveth to all men liberally, and upbraideth not, and it shall be given to him."* God's perspective is God's wisdom. We receive God's wise perspective through spending time in His Word so that it gets deep down in our hearts. Expect the best out of your life and out of your members. Expect them to give abundantly and to prosper abundantly. Expect them to change, mature and grow in the things of God. Your expectation will become your manifestation. So expect the extraordinary because you are an extraordinary woman!

Partnership & Mentoring

Keep your girlfriends!!! From your early or childhood days, as well as the friends that God connects you with along the way. Leading ladies need to develop and maintain solid covenant partnerships with other leading ladies and powerful women of God! I have actively pursued maintaining my friendships with friends that I have had in my life since elementary school. Some of them have become successful businesswomen, some Pastor's wives and some are dominating as working wives and mothers. But the most important thing is that no matter how full our schedules become, we always make time to chat by phone, e-mail or meet with each other during our travels across the country.

Don't become a "loner". Remember that your friends love you and want the best for you. You must believe and expect the best from them and continually trust God to be able to maintain your friendships. Even within the ministry, the Lord will help you identify some ladies that are mature enough to separate your friendship from the anointing on your life as their Pastor. However, you must be careful with this because it takes an extreme amount of maturity not to become familiar or envious.

Also remember that no one, including you, is the "perfect friend"! You have to believe this and also be willing to accept some of their flaws. Imagine if we cut off every friend that we ever had because of an aggravating personality trait? We would all be friendless! You, as a woman, need to maintain those relationships. Our children also need to see long-term healthy friendships so they will know how to have balanced lives as well. Believe it or not, even our husbands enjoy seeing that we "have a life" outside of them and the ministry work that we do!

Always remember to mentor someone as a leading lady and to be mentored. Seek out mentors that have accomplished things at higher levels than you and yourself have achieved, and then glean from their anointing and knowledge. In order for the leading lady to accomplish great things, she must pursue those who have already blazed a trail ahead of her, and have gone beyond what she has accomplished.

When my husband and I first started pastoring, I asked God to allow me to meet and be mentored by women of God such as Pastor Taffi Dollar and Dr. Barbara Layton. I sought to be spiritually connected with someone greater than myself and what I had achieved in God. I realized that in order to get to their level, I was going to have to capture their anointing. I do this by continually listening to and sowing into these women of God through their messages on CD and through participation in their conferences. I understand that it is my covenant right to expect to receive the same anointing and blessing as that of my mentors. I am grateful for the deposit that I have received from these great women of God; God has truly blessed me and fulfilled my hearts desire to meet them. I will always desire the mentorship of women of God such as these, as well as mentor other leading ladies who are forthcoming. I believe that partnership and mentoring are some of the keys to fulfilling our destiny as God's leading ladies.

I have been blessed to enjoy being mentored by those who enjoy pastoring. As a result, I love to Pastor. I have a passion for it and cannot think of anything else I want to do more. Unfortunately, there are some leading ladies who do not feel this way. They are unhappy and feel trapped by the cares that they feel go along with being in leadership. But it is all about who you are connected to and mentored by. It's all a matter of perspective. Seeing your role as a burden is not the will of God for your life, leading lady!

Furthermore, you cannot allow people to control you, or to tell you what God's will is for your life. Be sure not to allow others to dictate to you who and what you are supposed to be. Some may feel that you should simply be quiet and silently support, but God may have called you to teach and minister to the public. Some may feel that you should act very reserved and dress with the traditional, "church hat", lap scarf and white gloves. But I don't dress in that style at all. In fact, most would compare my personal style of dress as trendy and contemporary. We have to feel comfortable knowing that we are entitled to our own style and expression of who we are. Be an individual and be yourself. You have your own anointing, given to you by God, not someone else. Be who GOD has called you to be!

Make a decision to surround yourself with happy Pastor's and Pastor's wives. All of the friends that Dr. Ben and I have that are in ministry, love God, love each other, love the people and love the ministry! This is such an encouragement to us and we all draw from each other. Don't try to make bonds with "nay-sayers" or those that believe that Pastoring is "doom and gloom". Seek out friends with whom you can share things in a healthy way, so that you have a release for your thoughts and feelings. Above all, allow your emotions to move you towards God, not away from Him! Make a daily, or even a moment-by- moment decision to be content at all times, no matter what is going on in your life. Every day is an appointment with destiny. Walk in the contentment, peace and security of God. Challenges will come, but the word says to be of good cheer, because we have overcome the world! Keep God's perspective!

The Leading Lady and Her Man of God

On a final and more intimate note, I want to talk about what we possess, the spirit of influence in our marriage and can literally make and mold our husband's by the words that we use and the attitude that we choose to embrace. Our words and attitude have so much power! We as our husband's helpmeet, which means we are to help him meet the vision and purpose that God has given him. Leading ladies are king producers. A woman who is secure and confident in her relationship with God builds a strong marriage partnership and family with her husband.

When I first met Dr. Ben, he was already an anointed musician and wonderful family man. He realized that the one thing he was missing was a woman of God to help pray through and bring out the many other gifts still inside of him! As a result of our marriage, we have increased exponentially.

I rely on the Holy Spirit daily to help me walk in wisdom and grace. A woman who is always unhappy and frustrated is not relying on the Holy Spirit. Look within and not without. Everyday I realize more and more how much I am dependent upon the Holy Spirit for grace, creativity and a fresh anointing. Leading lady, your relationship with God is primary, so that you can be an able minister to your husband, your children and your home.

The leading lady understands that while there is glamour associated with her position, it is balanced by hard work and sacrifice. She understands and embraces the responsibility of caring for the man of God and he in turn should pamper and take wonderful care of you and your children. You have the ability to do more than one thing and run an entire estate because with time you will learn how to use your planner to organize your weeks and delegate at high levels. Delegation is key. Remember that before you decide that you are "called" by God to start a worldwide ministry, dominate the dishes! In other words take care of your household as well. Keep first things first. You will need to assemble a team to help you prepare for travel, prepare meals, take care of the children, administrative duties and household. You have to delegate so you don't allow yourself to feel overwhelmed by the responsibility that God has entrusted you with. Just know that the bigger leader your man of God is, the bigger the responsibility. Therefore, prepare yourself by being organized and efficient, and keeping your spirit, mind, and body rested.

Also remember what we talked about earlier in the chapter, understanding the power of submission. Be willing to submit and accept your husband's instruction without debating or constantly questioning his decisions. Understand that even in times when he may be wrong, God will still honor and bless his decision because of his office. God will also give you wisdom on when and how to communicate with him effectively because you are his partner in life, ministry and business, so you do have a voice. With practice, you will be able to speak with clarity and boldness and learn to listen with an understanding heart.

Let's talk about keeping yourself together! You want to look, smell and feel your best at all times. This will require getting plenty of sleep, rest and exercise. This also means you need to be mindful of what you put into your body. Keep your weight down and take plenty of vitamins and consider juicing fresh fruits and vegetables daily so you will be able to do all that you are called to each day. I also recommend that you consider using a holistic doctor along with your medical physician to help create a healthy diet full of plenty of water, fresh fruits, vegetables and protein. Pamper yourself by keeping your hair, skin, nails and feet in order! You can stay current with the most recent fashion, hair and make up trends simply by picking up a magazine. It is so important that in 2005 you don't have a 1998 hairstyle! Let it go girl! Change is critical. Purge your closet at least once a year. Some outfits just look old, traditional and maternal. Regularly ask those closest to you for their advice on how you REALLY look to them and be open to change accordingly. I remember the time when I gained quite a bit of weight and went from a size 8 to a size 12, but when I wore my clothes, I still saw myself as an 8! However, my sisters had to help me by being completely honest with me and letting me know, "you're a 12 and you look like it!" Needless to say, until I shedded the extra pounds, I had to go out and make some major changes to my wardrobe. Keeping yourself together is essential for you and for your husband. Remember, no matter how anointed a man becomes; he is still moved by what he *sees*! Though you should not feel like you have to compete with other women or other women in the church, you still want to keep your edge. You should be at the top of your game spiritually, emotionally, financially and physically.

Also be sure that in your effort to be a firm leader,

that you also keep your softness and femininity. No matter how strong you become in ministry, always maintain your softness, youthfulness and beauty. Your husband still wants his wife to have a gentle, free spirit. Be able to laugh and maintain the "girlishness" he was so attracted to in the beginning. Make sure you and your man of God keep the passion and fire in your marriage! Make sure you are creative at home and in the "bedroom". Like my husband always says, Victoria isn't a secret in our home! Plan romantic retreats and get aways and continue to flirt with each other and just have a good time!

It is an awesome responsibility to have the mantle of leading lady, but through prayer and perspective, you are anointed to be all that God has called you to be! I encourage you to walk uprightly, pray in the Holy Spirit, speak your daily confessions and use the authority God has given you to have life of abundance. Make a "plan" for success and "decide" to be blessed. No matter how you start, what you presently do, how you finish is what counts! You can do it! Enjoy the adventure!

From the Heart of First Ladies

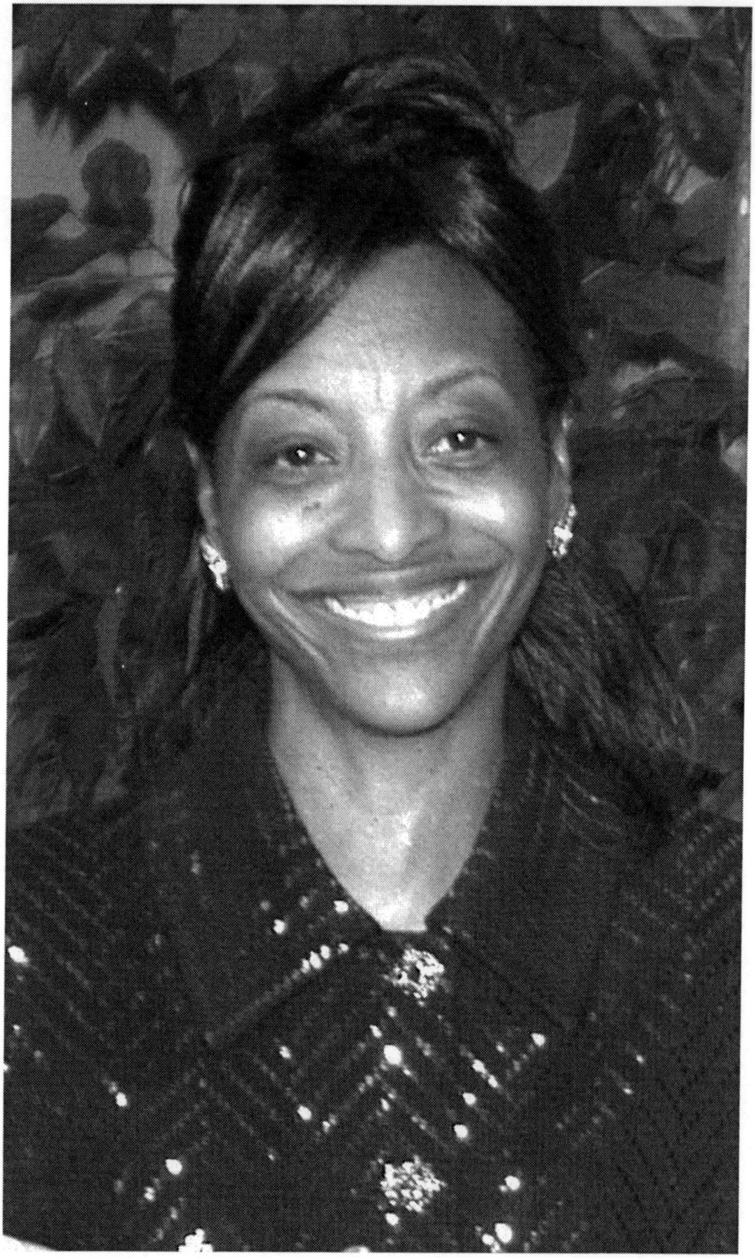

CHAPTER FIVE

FROM THE HEART OF
Pastor Barbara Easley

NEW LIFE CHRISTIAN FELLOWSHIP CHURCH
GOOSE CREEK, SOUTH CAROLINA

The Heart of a First Lady

When we first moved here from Atlanta, Georgia to Columbia, South Carolina, back in 1990, our bible study started in Charleston, South Carolina for a period of time. We taught Bible Study at a funeral home, a clubhouse, and then into our very own Church located in Goose Creek, South Carolina. I remember how God dealt with me about praying for my husband during this time.

Prior to moving to South Carolina my husband was an Evangelist. We both fell in love with the people of God, and the Lord moved tremendously in our lives. Many souls were saved, because of the love we both have for the Word of God. As the Lord spoke to my husband about coming to SC, fear fell upon my heart, and I began to meditate on scriptures of faith, such as " I can do all things through Christ Jesus who strengthens me", and " God has not given me a spirit of fear, but of power, love and a sound mind. The Lord spoke through a Pastor in Columbia SC that ministered to us. He told us that we would birth an Isaac not an Ishmael, (Gen 15:17-21) so don't be moved, because you both will go through some hard times, but be strong in the Lord, you are already equipped for ministry. From there we went to Charleston SC, without any money or savings. We had spent everything.

Genesis 15:17-21
v. 17 "And it came to pass, that, when the sun went down, and it was dark, behold a smoking furnace, and a burning lamp that passed between those pieces."

v. 18 "In the same day the Lord made a covenant with Abram, saying, Unto thy seed have I given this land, from the river of Egypt unto the great river, the river Eu-phra'tes:"

v. 19 "The Ken ites, and the Ken iz-zites, and the Kad'mon-ites,"

v. 20 "And the Hittites, and the Per iz-zites, and the Reph'a-ims,"

v. 21 "And the Amorites, and the Canaan-ites, and the Gir'ga-shites, and the Jeb'u-sites."

During this time my husband was working and doing Bible Study once a week, commuting back and forth from Columbia to Charleston. In 1991 a year later we moved to Charleston. I begin to remember about the raven feeding Elisha. I prayed one night, and the Lord said, "I will provide for you." During this time we didn't even have a refrigerator or any food. At this time we had 3 children. That night I said, "Lord you took care of Elisha, and you told us not to worry about what we shall eat or wear." God is so good! He used an unsaved lady that lived next door to us, to feed us for six months. We were so amazed and thankful. The lady prepared food for us that we didn't turn down, until about the fourth month. That's when pride happened for me. I felt like "how could we minister to her when she is feeding us?" So one night she had this large feast (each holiday), everything you could possible name to eat, she was from the Philippines. Her family was not saved so sometimes her husband and other family members would be drunk, so she would always bring the food over to us. Well this particular night she wanted us to come over, and I said. "I was not going over there because I was tired of her paying and preparing our food." That's when the Lord dealt with me, and said I was operating in pride. I then went over to her house (because it wasn't like I was fasting), and during this time we were also able to minister to her and she respected us highly.

During this time we didn't have a working car. The children and I had to walk to the store sometimes to purchase food. I remember once someone tried to run us over in a car. Not only were my husband and I going through hard times, but our children also. In 1993 my husband was laid off his job, so we had to move in to low-income apartment, which was the first time. We never stopped paying our tithes and offering. A Pastor once asked us "How could we do this with all that we were going through?" It amazed him to see what the Lord was doing with us even through hard times. I also home schooled our children, which

I enjoyed a lot. The school system in the area we lived in was not that great. We also applied for food stamps, and shopped at the thrift store for our clothes, (we ate good, and I was able to bless a lot of people in the community with different recipes) and it gave me an opportunity to share Jesus Christ with them. It felt kind of embarrassing when you've never done this before, but the Lord ministered to me one night when I was praying and God reminded me about the time when I was a little girl and my parents lived in section 8 apartments, so did my husband as a child. We were happy on some occasions, and we didn't know we were poor. At times the Lord continued to have me Thank and Praise Him! Rejoice in the Lord always Rejoice! For everything He is doing in our lives. The scripture Matthew 6:33 became alive in my spirit. I know we had been seeking the kingdom of God diligently, so I knew He was going to bless us eventually more. During the winter, one night, our son Dexter Jr., almost died. He had a high fever and we thought it was just the flu. We found out he was having a seizure, and we rushed him to the hospital. We made it just in time. The doctors said he could have died if we hadn't made it to the hospital. God is truly Jehovah Rapha in our lives. I told the devil "you will not have our son; he belongs to God, and he will live." I prayed Psalms 91:1-15 in the Holy Ghost, until I felt peace in my spirit.

Psalms 91:1-15
v. 1 "He that dwelleth in the secret place of the most High shall abide under the shadow of the Almighty."

v. 2 "I will say of the Lord, He is my refuge and my fortress: my God; in him will I trust."

v. 3 "Surely he shall deliver thee from the snare of the fowler, and from the noisome pestilence."

v. 4 "He shall cover thee with his feathers, and under his wings shalt thou trust: his truth shall be thy shield and buckler."

v. 5 "Thou shalt not be afraid for the terror by night: nor for the arrow that flieth by day:"

v. 6 "Nor for the pestilence that walketh in darkness; nor for the destruction that wasteth at noonday."

v. 7 "A thousand shall fall at thy side, and ten thousand at thy right hand; but it shall not come nigh thee."

v. 8 "Only with thine eyes shalt thou behold and see the reward of the wicked."

v. 9 "Because thou hast made the Lord, which is my refuge, even the most High, thy habitation;"

v. 10 "There shall no evil befall thee, neither shall any plague come nigh thy dwelling."

v. 11 "For he shall give his angels charge over thee, to keep thee in all thy ways."

v. 12 "They shall bear thee up in their hands, lest thou dash thy foot against a stone."

v. 13 "Thou shalt tread upon the lion and adder: the young lion and the dragon shalt thou trample under feet."

v. 14 "Because he hath set his love upon me, therefore will I deliver him: I will set him on high, because he hath known my name."

v. 15 "He shall call upon me, and I will answer him: I will be with him in trouble; I will deliver him, and honour him."

We encountered something we never thought would happen. We decided to move into a larger building. The man we thought owned the building really didn't, but we didn't find out until after we were paying him the rent money to use the building for Bible Study, "big mistake". My husband was so upset and discouraged he said, "That's it, we are leaving up out of South Carolina, the people are right, there are demons here; Barbara let's leave." I was also shocked from what this man had done to us. He used us to steal a great amount of money from the original owner. The next day we went to Columbia, South Carolina and found an apartment. Dexter got a job at a car dealership, and I was going back to my old job at a day care center. After we returned home that night, and we were about to go to bed, the Lord spoke to me so strongly about not leaving Charleston, South Carolina. On the next day I shared this with my husband "baby we can't leave, we must obey God. We don't want to birth an Ishmael, but an Issac." My husband was very quiet.

The next day my husband told me to call the office of the apartment building that we had put our deposit on (first and last months rent), and tell them we changed our mind. As we did this, the Lord birthed New Life Christian Fellowship Church on October 8, 1995. We began to have Bible Study in our home during the week and Sunday service in the clubhouse. We started with our family of six people and a gentleman who worked with Pastor Dexter (Willie Smith) who is still a faithful member. During this time I began to call forth the people from the north, south, east and west. No one was there, except our family, and Willie Smith, which is now a Minister at our church. Sometimes Minister Willie would look as if he were saying, "When are they coming?"

Mark 10:29-30 "And whatever we give up for the gospel sake shall return to us a hundredfold here and on earth and heaven, because we were obedient." God changed me, I began to wake up in the middle of the night and would pray and pray. I started searching scriptures about people who use to pray a lot. I found many names in the bible I never heard of myself, that satisfied me. I felt like that's what the Lord called me to do. I begin to ask my husband "would it be alright if we could pray before each service, and before Bible Study?" Later after this had taken place Pastor Dexter decided to have a prayer night once a week. In 1996 I taught my first prayer class to five ladies in our church. The Lord begin to bless tremendously. I noticed that members begin to have a love for prayer, and our church really flourished because of the result of prayer.

Mark 10:29-30
v. 29 "And Jesus answered and said, Verily I say unto you. There is no man that hath left house, or brethren, or sisters, or father, or mother, or wife, or children, or lands, for my sake, and the gospel's."

v. 30 "But he shall receive an hundredfold now in this time, houses, and brethren, and sisters, and mothers, and children, and lands, with persecutions; and in the world to come eternal life."

I also enjoy ministering to the women of God at our church. I'm excited about sharing the word of God with them; I'm real, practical, and transparent. Another ministry I enjoy is sign language. I started doing a lot in all the ministries at NLCF Church, and as a result of all of this the Lord is really blessing us a lot! We no longer live in a small house, like the one we once had 1600 square ft. The Lord also used someone to bless us with 400,000 dollars, which was a shock to me, and Pastor. Then the Lord told us to give the 400,000 all back to the Kingdom of God. We obeyed God! The Lord reminded me of Solomon, and how he sought for wisdom and the Lord blessed him tremendously. A year later the Lord blessed us with a 4900 square foot home! We then turned around and blessed Minister Willie and his family with a home! We blessed our secretary with a car, and blessed others with money, and other things that God has told us to do. But God is always first, and as the ministry continued to grow we began to travel a lot. I was so excited about what God was doing in our lives. I begin to do even more in the ministry as my husband begin to travel more.

Although loving the Lord and having a desire to support my Husband in the work of the ministry, there were situations that occurred, that I was not prepared for. As a result of not being prepared, my physical body experienced challenges due to stress in the ministry. I was not able to do a lot, because of being too rigid.

The church grew and I started doing everything in several different ministries, instead of delegating. Just to name a few:

- Sign Language Ministry
- Women's Fellowship
- Prayer
- Altar Counselor Ministry
- Director of the Church Academy
- Outreach Ministry
- Counseling 3 times per week

    I was involved with so much there was just no time for caring for myself or relaxation, due to the responsibilities. It was overwhelming and stressful. I started speaking negative and painful words to my husband, as well as others. I remember feeling like I just wanted "out" of the ministry, because of shame and guilt, along with what my body started going through. As a result of stress my body shut down. I found out after a certain period of time, through a specialist doctor, my ovaries had deteriorated, and this is when my health complications began. I started losing weight, and my behavior pattern was out of character. My husband, was the first to notice what was happening, and he seeing me go through this, never changed his compassion towards me; he just stood in faith. Dr. Colbert (Specialist Doctor) that was recommended to us, gave me a lot of advise on how to properly care for myself; taking natural supplements, eating healthy (natural foods), exercise, confessing the word, and listening to comedy. As I started to follow his advice I realized that I needed to discipline my body, so I sat down 1 year from activities of the ministry, in order to do this. During that time I studied, confessed the word, and listen to my husband tapes that ministered to me on faith; renewing the mind, healing scriptures, resting spiritually, and mentally. Also during this time my husband, Dr. Bridget Hilliard, and my sister Nadine encouraged me a lot as I was going through these challenges.

"Enjoying Life: The Best Thing That Ever Happened To Me"

Now that the Lord has healed my body! Hallelujah! I am very joyful, vibrant and enjoying life, like never before. I thank God for healing my body and obeying natural things like eating the right foods, spiritual and natural, as well as feeling great and excited about ministry again! I respect my Godly patient, loving man of faith; my husband who stood in faith for my healing. (I LOVE HIM SOOO MUCH!!!) I have a love for people like never before. Currently I'm only on a few ministries. I enjoy life, relax more, laugh more, I enjoy riding the motorcycle with my husband, taking walks, working out three days a week, and I don't take life so seriously. I take naps daily; and we now have someone assist with cooking and housekeeping for us. Praise God! I can just be myself!

God is just so good! I LOVE YOU LORD! THANK YOU FOR HEALING MY BODY! MY MIND AND LIVING ABUNDANTLY! As a result of this I now eat all healthy foods!

To Pastor's Encouragement

I encourage Pastors wives to be themselves, meditate on scriptures (Proverbs to me has been such a blessing for everyday life), and faith scriptures. Begin believing in your heart that you are the most beautiful person God has created and that you are fearfully and wonderfully made). Don't take life so seriously, enjoy life. Jesus wants us to have life, and life more abundantly. Relax, listen to some nice Christian music, take a walk, pamper yourself weekly, and don't compare yourself with anyone it's not wise. You are unique first in the eyes of God and in the people who you impact with your life. We are called to make disciples by teaching the word of God, not so much behind the pulpit but with our lives. Let's encourage each other not to look at our faults or shortcomings, but to be a blessing, and encouragement to everyone. We need each other! I'm abiding in Him! I have joy unspeakable!

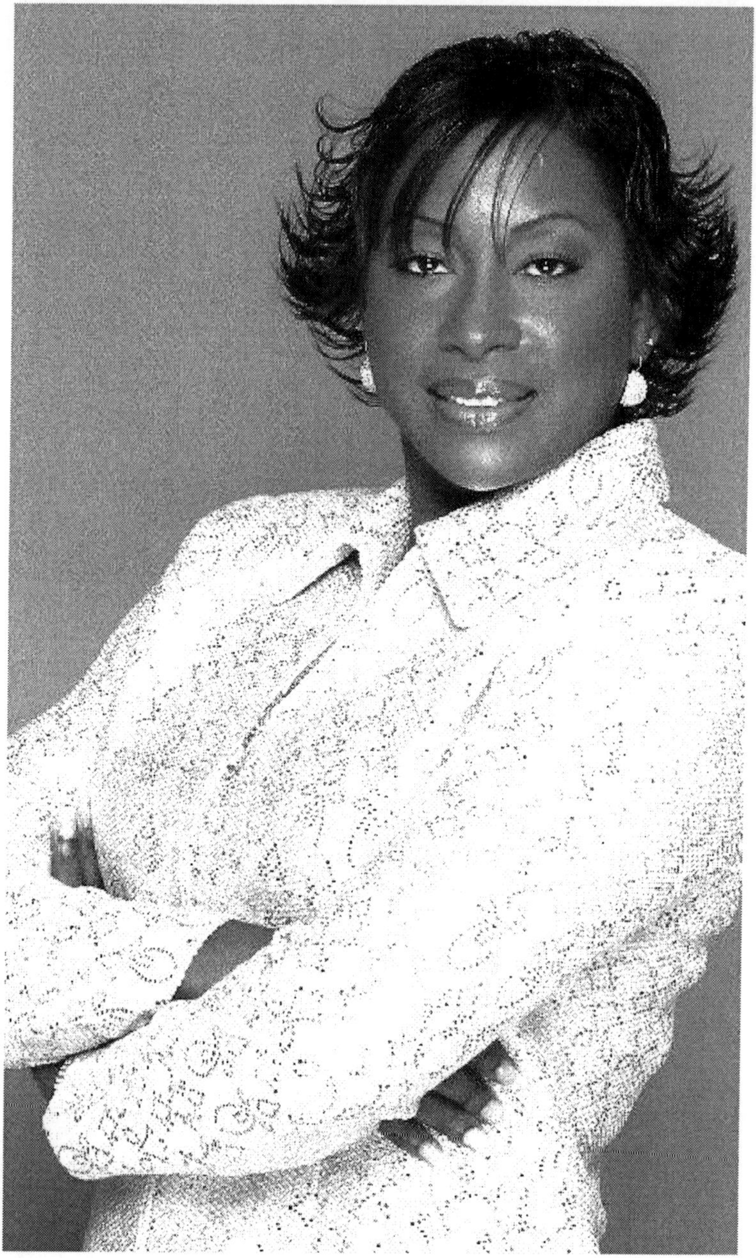

CHAPTER SIX

FROM THE HEART OF
Dr. Angela Manning

NEW LIFE MINISTRIES
VALDOSTA, GEORGIA

The Heart of a First Lady

My best encounter as a First Lady at the beginning of our ministry was when my husband, Bishop Larry Manning, and I were celebrating our third Pastor and Wife Appreciation. I had been and still was going through a lot with some of the members. On this particular night there was a prophetess visiting our church. She prophesied to me that God was going to send me some handmaidens to assist me. God knew what I was going through and He was sending me some women to be my armor bearers. I started out with five, and they were good for a season, but the one that was truly called to serve me is still serving today. The others dwindled off one by one. Being a pastor's wife is a lonely position some times, but to know that God cares enough to assign some one to you to make things easier for you is a blessing.

My best encounter as a first lady after about seven years into the ministry was when the deacons finally realized and accepted me for who I am. They realized that I was not just your traditional first lady, but I was called to help my husband in ministry. Some times it's hard to let go of something that you have been taught for years. My husband is not a traditional pastor so of course his wife is not traditional either. Everything began to flow much better then.

My worst encounter as a First Lady would be

when my husband founded the church, which was in 1991. Prior, to that I had been a minister's wife for nine years. Let me just say that being a minister's wife was a piece of cake compared to being a Pastor's wife; when my husband became a pastor that put me in a whole different ball game. So being in this new role as a pastor's wife, of course I wanted everyone to like me. I found out very quickly that wasn't going to happen. I couldn't figure out why not. I was good looking (still is), I dressed stylish (still do), out going personality, sense of humor, but no matter how perfect you might be, church members will always find something wrong with the pastor's wife. There were many times I would cry to my husband saying I couldn't do it anymore. One time I told him he needed to find him another wife, because this one has had enough. There were a couple of sisters who said that I wasn't friendly because I didn't speak to them or their children. In my effort to prove that I was friendly, I found myself running after people even when they were driving away to make sure I had spoken to them. After a few Sundays of that I realized that there is only one of me and many of them and if they wanted me to speak to them they needed to come to me.

Another occasion was when the women planned a retreat and one of the ladies said to me, I hope I like you better after this retreat. The Holy Ghost arrested me and would not let me say what I wanted to say, so I smiled and said, I hope you like me better too. You can imagine what I really wanted to say.

Those were just a couple of my worst encounters, but there are many more in the beginning of the ministry. Now, I thank God for everything I went through because every encounter made me into the bold woman of God I am today. Those encounters helped process me for my purpose. Let the record show that today I will not tolerate anyone in the church talking to me that way.

My advice to a First Lady would be to always be yourself and don't allow the people to change you into what they think a First Lady should be. Don't be a people pleaser just please the Lord. Get delivered from people so that what they say or think about you don't affect you. Be confident in who you are realizing that nobody can be a better First Lady to your husband than you can. Know that you are the best looking, best dressing, and best pastor supporting woman in the church. Pray for your husband and if possible be there every time he has to preach, whether it's at his church or not. Be able to spiritually discern. A First Lady needs to have holy boldness as well a Godly compassion. Make sure that the congregation knows that you and your husband love cherish and are devoted to each other. Never become best friends with any of the members in your church. Never discuss anything negative about your marriage with any member of your church. Never allow the members of your church to become familiar with you. The members should treat you with the same respect as they do the pastor. Don't allow yourself to get so attached to any of the members so that when they turn their backs or walk away and leave the church you end up with a broken heart. It's the one you help the most who will leave you. You've got to know when to hold them and you've got to know when to fold them. Stay in love with your husband, love the Lord, and help your husband feed the sheep.

The Pastor's wife is the first lady of the church that her husband pastors. She is the spiritual mother to all who comes under the leadership of her husband. The pastor's wife sets the standard for the women in the church. She is the example for the women to follow. The pastor's wife needs to be well versed in the Scriptures so that she can give godly counsel from the word of God to those who come to her. The first lady should be active in her husband's ministry. She doesn't necessarily have to be a preacher, but she should be actively involved in some ministry in the church. She needs to be visible. The members need to see that she is a part of what her husband, the pastor, is doing. She should be his biggest fan who is always in his corner. The pastor's wife needs affirmation from her husband from the pulpit. When the members hear the pastor say good things about his wife, the first lady, they will respect her more. The first lady is more than just the pastor's wife. Her name is not Pastor so and so's wife. She has a name. She has an identity. She is more than just the pastor's wife.

"Pastor's Wife's Declaration"

My husband is my pastor
I am his wife
I am who I am by the grace of God
I am submitted by choice
I am committed by calling
I am supportive by my prayers and my presence
I am anointed for my position
I am intelligent
I am creative
I am virtuous
No one else can be a wife to my husband like I can
I am excited about who I am and what I do
I am more than a Pastor's Wife

By: Dr. Angela S. Manning

*From the Heart
of
First Ladies*

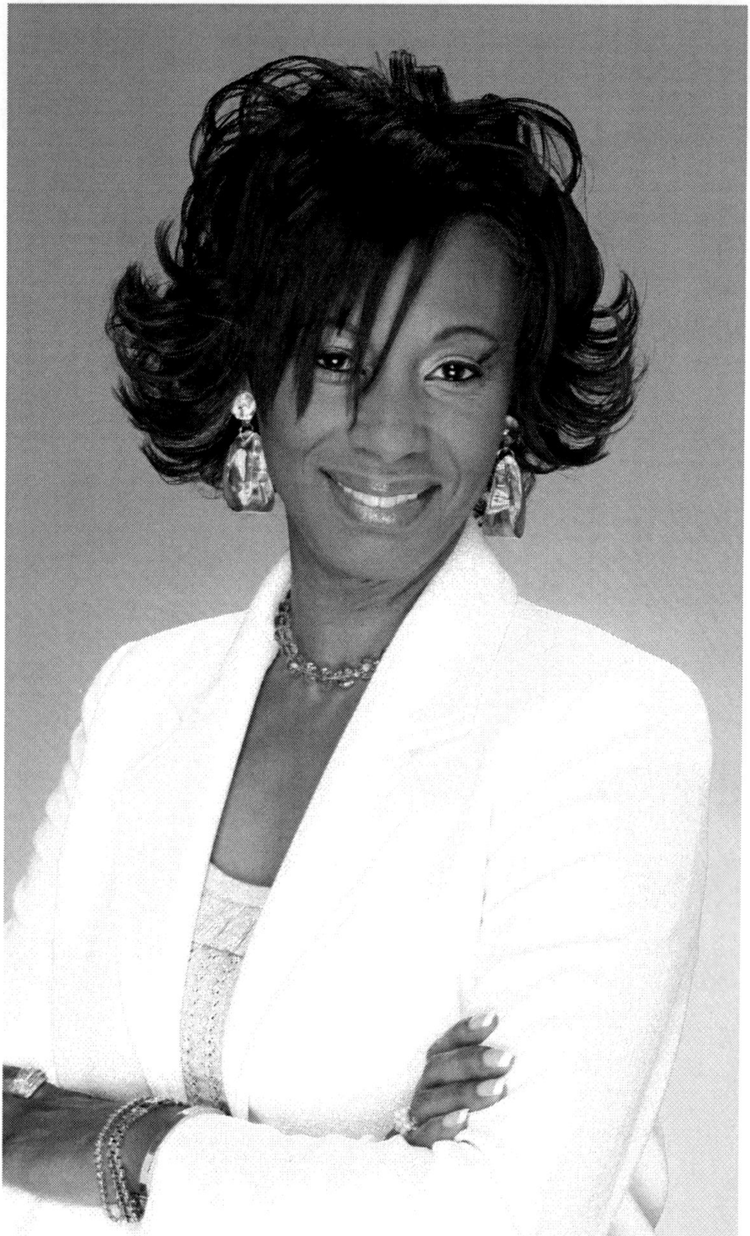

CHAPTER SEVEN

FROM THE HEART OF
Elder Anita Jackson

UNITED CHRISTIAN MINISTRIES
GREER, SOUTH CAROLINA

The Heart of a First Lady

"He Came To Himself"

In Luke chapter fifteen is the familiar story of the prodigal son. In this story there are three stages of the younger son who left his father. There is the stage of rebellion, repentance and rejoicing. The first stage: Rebellion. The younger son went to a far away country (Verses 11-16). According to the Jewish law the older son who stayed home would receive twice as much as the younger son (Deuteronomy 21:17) and a father could distribute his wealth during his lifetime as he wished. Keep in mind it was the older son who stayed home. The older son was a hard worker but his "Labor of love" did please his father. Because like the Prophet Jonah, he did God's will but not from his heart (Jonah 4; Ephesians 6:6). So, it was perfectly legal for the younger son to ask for his share of the estate and even to sell it; but it certainly would not be a loving thing to do. If the son sold it; it would be like saying to his father, "I wish you were dead."

We are always heading for trouble whenever we value things more than people, pleasure more than duty, and distant things more than the blessings we have right at home. Remember, prosperity, follows order. Jesus warned two disputing brothers. "Take heed and beware of covetousness!" (Luke 12:15) The covetous person can never be satisfied, no matter how much he acquires and a dissatisfied heart leads to a disappointed life.

The prodigal son is learned the hard way, just like most of us; you can enjoy things money can buy. But don't ignore things money cannot buy. Money cannot buy you peace of mind, love in your home or the joy of the Lord (Galatians 5:22). The far country in our story does not necessarily mean a distant place. The far country represents your heart, meaning that you are back from God. God never moved. You did. You are not waiting on God. God is waiting on you to return back to Him. Life away from God is never what you expect.

The prodigal son resources ran out. His friends ran out. A famine came and the younger son was forced to do for a stranger what he would never have to do for his own father. He had to work in a bad environment. This story is the Lord's way of emphasizing what sin really does in the lives of those who reject the father's will. Sin promises freedom but it always brings slavery. John 8:34 tells us whoever commits sin is a slave of sin. Sin promises success but it always bring failure. Sin promises life but eventually brings death. "The wages of sin is death but the gift of God is eternal life" (Romans 6:23).

The younger son thought he would "Find himself" but he only lost himself. When God is left out of our lives, enjoyment becomes enslavement. But here is the key to our story, "Repentance." He came to himself. In Colossians 1:13, The Greek term for "Deliver" means to draw to one's self or to rescue." To repent means, "To change one's mind," and that's exactly what the younger man did is he cared for pigs, he came to himself while feeding and eating with the pigs.

When I say, "He came to himself," this suggests that up to this point he had not really been himself. What is it going to take before you come to yourself? Come out of the pigpens of this world! You have a Heavenly Father who is waiting to embrace and love you. The younger son changed his mind about himself and his situation, and he recognized that he was more than that! He confessed that his father was a generous man and that his service at home was far better than the bondage in the far country. It is God's goodness, not man's badness that leads us to repentance (Romans 2:4).

The third and final stage of our story is, "Rejoicing." The younger son could see his father at distance, but he knew it was his father. This where the song "Oh happy day," come into play. The father and the son took out running towards one another. The father welcomed his son and everybody stopped what they were doing to watch this scene. The father ordered his workers to kill the fattest and the finest calf that he owned because a reunion and a party was about to take place. Notice something in this scene;

the father didn't fuss at his son. Because he was a wise man and he knew his son's healing was going to come through his love for his son.

When someone returns to the Lord don't fuss at them just love them. Our Heavenly Father is rich in His mercy and grace and great in His love toward them (Ephesians 2:1-10). Our return to our Heavenly Father is possible because of the sacrifice of His Son on the cross. No matter what some preachers or singers may claim. We are saved by the sacrifice of His Son on the cross. Some years ago in my life, I like the prodigal son, God had to allow me to get to my lowest point. I thought the grass was greener on the other side. Yes, I was saved and I knew I was saved but I went back on God. But the good news is I came to myself. I am talking to someone who needs to know that there is life for you after the far country experience. Forget about yesterday! Philippians 3:13 reminds us to "Press!" Paul goes on to say in Colossians, "Who has delivered us from the power of darkness." The enemy tried to kill me, but God rescued me! "The thief comes to steal kill and destroy, but I come that you may have life and have it more abundantly." (John 10:10)

Claim your inheritance. God said, "I was married to a backslider. I'm knocking at your door. Come back to Me! You don't have to remain as you are. Come to yourself!" God is telling you to come out of the situation. What are you doing in that strange place?

Hanging out with that crowd? Why are you putting stuff in God's temple that shouldn't be? Why are you drinking alcohol? God wants to deliver and rescue you. God is calling you to come back to Him. Our God is a God of order and He is calling you back to Him.

One of the problems we have in the church today is when someone comes forward to confess their sins (James 5:16; 1 John 1:9) many in the church act as if they cannot believe it. The next time that somebody looks at you after you give your testimony, tell them to look in the mirror themselves, because God wants to deliver people from their stuff. Sometimes you have to go through before you can get to! God will allow you to go through hell in order for you to help somebody else. We must pray and love one another. No greater love than this than a Man to lay down His life for His friends.

I give Him honor and praise! Because He's worthy of praise! He's still healing and delivering. I give Him glory! Don't you allow anybody to put you down or pull you down! The Devil should have never let me find out what God has for me! The Lord said, "I will give you houses that you did not build, vineyards that you did not plant and wells that you did not dig!" But your faith has got to go get it! Paul said, "And if you are Christ's, then you are heirs according to the promise." (Galatians 3:29) We are not equal heirs which means half and half, but joint heirs. Joint heirs means all that Christ has is mine, and all that I have is His. At

Calvary I brought my sin and He gave me the riches of Abraham. I brought my sickness and He gave me health and healing. I brought my sin and He gave me total forgiveness. I brought my rejection and He adopted me into the family of God.

While writing this chapter I was struggling with what I should write. Not knowing what to write the Holy Spirit spoke to me and told me to look out my dining room window. God asked me, "What do you see?" And I responded, "A Crate Myrtle tree." He asked, "What else do you see?" I said to my self, "God is giving me a fresh revelation of what I should write." I went on to notice that on the Crate Myrtle tree there were pink flowers on it, with small green bulbs, and the leaves were changing to a yellow-orange color. And about that time the wind began to blow.

So I say to you Women of God, what God revealed to me while watching a Crate Myrtle tree from my dining room. As I watched the wind blowing it is a reminder that God's Holy Spirit continues to move within us. The pink bloom represents that you are beautiful in Christ. The bulb represents that you will continue to produce more fruit. The changing of the leaves represents God is taking you into another season all because you like the prodigal son came to yourself.

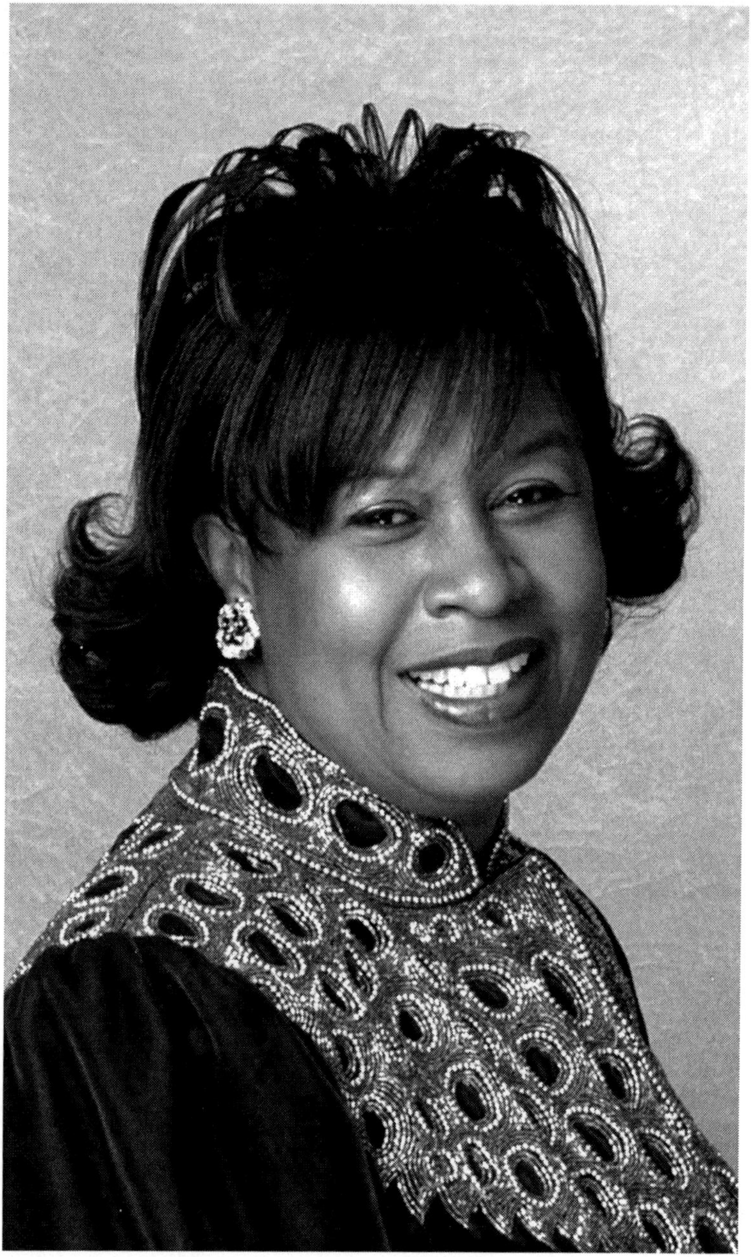

CHAPTER EIGHT

From the Heart of

Evangelist Carol Caldwell

First Baptist World Changers
International Ministries
Detroit, Michigan

The Heart Of A First Lady

My Most Favorable Experience As A First Lady

My most favorable experience as a First Lady is in the area of humility and submission. Often my husband, the Pastor would not release me to do many things that I desired and felt that I was called and qualified to do. These things included counseling, or taking a leadership role in certain areas and even him personally taking advice or listening to me. Feelings of hurt, intimidation, inferiority and even embarrassment tried to overtake me. However, I trusted Gods Word, that says, he that humble yourself under the mighty hand of God and in due time he shall exalt you. We don't always understand why people do what they do. However, we should not allow ourselves to feel any less because of their actions, but trust God and make full proof of your ministry as Paul writes to Timothy. Neither should we usurp authority and do what we think we are big and bad enough to do. But study, pray and continue to allow God to work on you. It may have nothing to do with you and everything to do with the other person. Maybe that person has some baggage or problem that tries to work against you. Or maybe it does have something to do with you and you really do need some work. What ever the case, stay humble and submit. However, in my case I later realized that my husband was trying to protect me and maybe himself from possibly operating in error. As I continued to be humble, and to study and pray God began to exalt me not only in the eyes of people but my husband's eyes. People began to approach me for a word not only at church but everywhere I went. Apostle Paul did say do the work of an evangelist. Even my husband began to take note of the words of wisdom I spoke and my powerful prayer life. Yes, even your husband is watching your life. Now he sends people to me. You see the answer is in the word. A man's head is Christ and he wants to hear from Him. Your man of God will take note to you when you speak the things that God speaks or when you sound like God. Nathan sent Bathsheba in to warn David of problems in the Kingdom when he was on his death bed. I King 1:11-22. We often have discernment of things and want our husbands to hear us but they sometimes won't. As she spoke to David, the prophet Nathan came in to confirm every word. When we speak the words of God, our husbands will recognize these words as Gods words and take heed. Not only that but, God will confirm every word. My sheep know my voice and a stranger he will not obey! Lets not make the mistake that Eve made and speak the things of Satan to our people and our husbands causing disaster, but let us always speak the things of God.

1 Kings 1:11-22
v. 11 "Wherefore Nathan spake untoBath-she-ba the mother of Solomon, saying, Hast thou not

heard that Ad-o-ni jah the son of Hag gith doth reign, and David our Lord knoweth it not?"

v. 12 "Now therefore come, let me, I pray thee, counsel, that thou mayest save thine own life, and the life of thy son Solomon."

v. 13 "Go and get thee in unto king David, and say unto him, Didst not thou, my lord, O king, swear unto thine handmaid, saying, Assurely Solomon thyson shall reignafter me, and he shall sit upon my throne? Why then doth Ad-o-ni jah reign?"

v. 14 "Behold, while thou yet talkest there with the king, I, also will come in after thee, and confirm thy words."

v. 15 "And Bath-she-ba went in unto the king into the chamber: and the king was very old; and Ab i-shag the Shu-nam-mite ministered unto the king."

v. 16 "And Bath-she-ba bowed, and did obeisance unto the king. And the king said, What wouldest thou?"

v. 17 "And she said unto him, My lord, thou swarest by the Lord thy God unto thine handmaid, saying, Assurely Sol-omon thy son shall reign after me, and he shall sit upon my throne."

v. 18 "And now, behold, Ad-o-ni jah reigneth; and now, my lord the king, thou knowest it not."

v. 19 "And he hath slain oxen and fat cattle and sheep in abundance, and hath called all the sons of the king, and A-bi a-thar the priest, and Jo-ab the captain of the host: but Solomon thy servant hath he not called."

v. 20 "And thou, my lord, O king, the eyes of all Israel are upon thee, that thou shouldest tell them who shall sit on the throne of my lord the king after him."

v. 21 "Otherwise it shall come to pass, when my lord the king shall sleep with his fathers, that I and my son Solomon shall be counted offenders."

v. 22 "And, lo, while she yet talked with the king, Nathan the prophet also came in."

My most unfavorable experience as a First Lady:

My most unfavorable experience as First Lady was when I was experiencing some test and trials with a few members in the congregation concerning myself and my children. A few people were loving the Pastor and not his wife and children. One day when another accusation was being made against one of my children, I was fed up, let my guard down and told the person "You don't have the Pastors Spirit at all" Although , this may not seem bad at all, It became offensive to that person as well as some of the members. I think I surprised them and probably frightened some of them. Here is what the Spirit of the Lord caused me to realize. First of all, people are often just that-**people.** We are lights and cannot always expect them to act or be what they should or to be where we are spiritually. Maybe she felt she was right. Maybe she was and I perceived her wrong. It was a time of testing and trials for me. Whatever the case, we are the lights and examples. Even when they may not be. This was therefore offensive to the person and many others. We must realize that some things babes can't handle and the maturity level of the congregation must always be considered. So we must always be wise and harmless (This was years ago and we've all grown in the Spirit tremendously.) This became an opportunity for Satan and several turned on me. I felt like David and had to really encourage myself, not really understanding what the people was experiencing.

I repented for offending the person and others. I immediately went before the congregation and apologized to bring healing to the matter. Blessed are the peace makers. This wasn't an easy thing to do and I didn't totally understand at the time. Today, the entire congregation loves me unconditionally. (and there were some that always did). I have no first lady issues or problems. I didn't totally understand what God was doing at that time. But he began to do something great in me for my humility. I first learned that God waits and judges every matter and I don't have to; the scales are in his hand. I learned to encourage myself as David when many turned on him. I learned what Jesus felt when he was treated and numbered as a transgressor when he wasn't one. (They were more disappointed with me than with the other person.) I also felt like what the woman caught in the very act felt like. This all brought about some resurrection power in me as I developed a greater love, compassion and understanding of people whether they are right or wrong.. The devil meant if for evil but God meant it for good. Oh, by the way, that other person and myself reconciled as God orchestrated it.

My advice to you is that if you have made a mistake or you are having problems in the congregation, trust God, follow what he leads you to do, stay humble, always love his people regardless of what they do and allow him to show you how to bring healing to the matter for both you and them.. I know there are different circumstances but the Lord will show you what to do in your case. It may be a different resolution. But, remember always follow peace. An unfavorable experience can become a most favorable one.

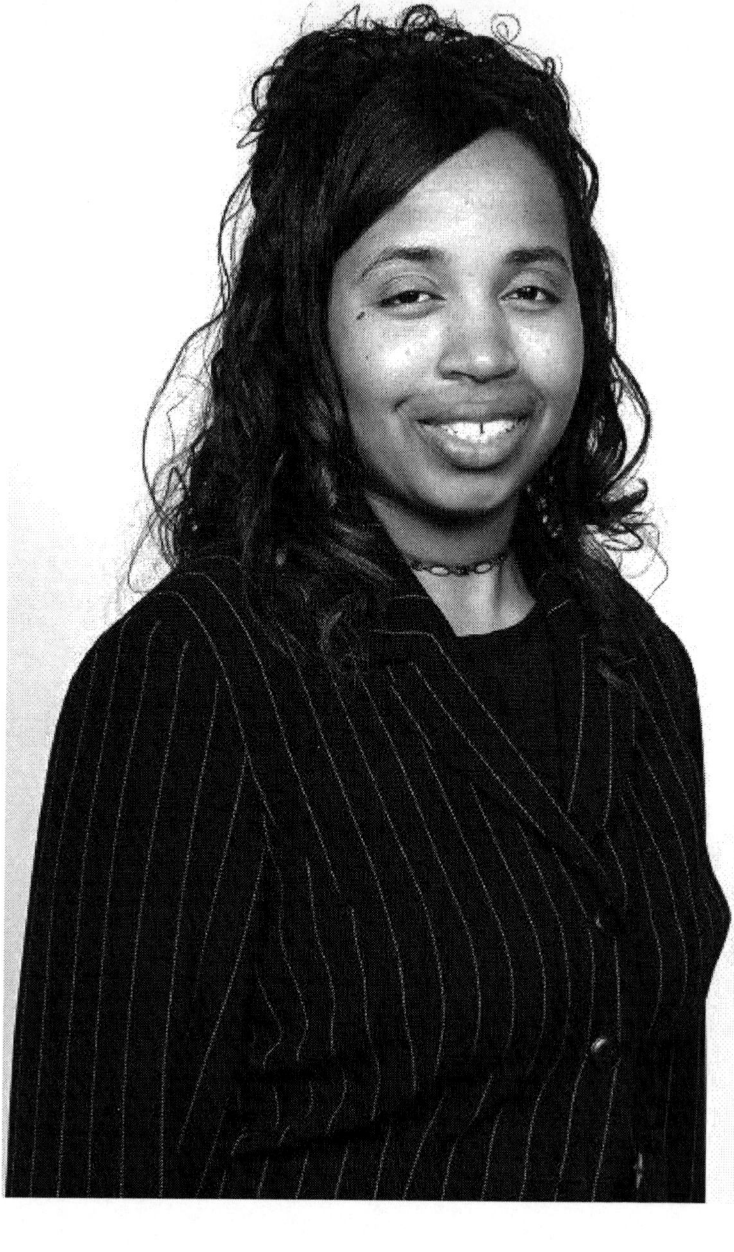

CHAPTER NINE

FROM THE HEART OF
Dr. Tracy Pickett

NEW JERUSALEM MISSIONARY
BAPTIST CHURCH
JACKSON, MISSISSIPPI

The Heart of a First Lady

A Pastor's Wife – The First Lady? What Did You Call Me?

Yes, I am a pastor's wife – what most refer to as a First Lady. Admittedly, this is a title I did not want to be called. In the beginning, I cringed each and every time someone called me F _ _ _ _ L _ _ _. During this time the definition I had of a first lady was based on my skewed perception of pastor's wives I had observed along the way. In my mind, a first lady was unapproachable, polished, 'holy', aloof, always immaculately groomed, the trophy wife placed on a pedestal without her permission, and so on. She seemed unreal to me or phony. Well, I was not perfect and I was certainly no phony! I did not want to be put on a pedestal. I knew who I really was. So, I would in my naiveté politely request that no one called me that. This was done in an effort to be humble. "Just call me Tracy," I would insist because that was fine with me. I was young.

God through Jesus and the Holy Spirit taught me how to be a pastor's wife. He revealed to me the definition that fit my role as my husband's wife. Notice that I said MY role as MY husband's wife. I am convinced that each pastor's wife is unique and divinely defined by God to fulfill His purpose through His chosen pastor's shepherding of His people.

What God Has Taught Me

My husband has been a pastor now for almost ten years. Over this time period, God has been revealing to me what it means to be a pastor's wife for my husband and God's people. I will attempt to give the partial list I know about at this point (God is still teaching me). A pastor's wife is (1) first of all a wife as defined in the Bible – his helper, (2) both a believer and a true disciple of Jesus Christ (I don't want to take anything for granted), and (3) a servant-leader. As your husband's helper, you must be able and prepared to help him in every way possible.

The Pastor's WIFE

By Design

God designed woman to be man's wife. Ladies, you are a wife to him first and foremost. You are his FIRST LADY. In Genesis 2:20b – 25, I learned that I was made to fill a void in my husband's life. God made me to be his number one helper. God made me for him to help him, not run him, in every way possible. I accepted this without disdain. God had confirmed to me over and over again that this is one of my main purposes in life. God has made us one. Unlike the world, 1 + 1 = 1 in God's Kingdom. God is awesome. Not only am I his FIRST LADY, but his only lady in the eyes of God.

Virtuous Woman

God further instructed me to be a virtuous woman as outlined in Proverbs 31:10-31. Here I am learning (God is teaching and I am applying with His help) from this passage that my character is to be noble and genuinely so. This means that my husband should be fully confident in me as his helpmate. My goal should never be to harm him but to be good to him. I am to work with him to maintain the household. I am to show compassion to the poor and the needy, both physically and spiritually, which are those we serve. My compassion should not be confined to my heart but should be revealed in action. Domestic responsibilities are to be exemplary from the dressing of the family to the home décor to my personal adornment (It's okay to look good). I should not ensnare the respect of my husband as his wife. I must respect him (Ephesians 5:33b). I am to be strong, spiritually having strength, dignity, wisdom and control over my tongue as I teach others. (Side note: Ladies we know that we can make or break our men by what we say with our tongue. Let us speak life into them instead of death (Proverbs 18:21). I know this can be challenging, especially when it is not reciprocated like we want it to be. Yet, it is a must). I am to take care of my home and not to be a busybody given to gossip. I am to be an outstanding mother and wife in the eyes of my children and husband, who really know me. I am to fear God. Whew! I got carried away. Excuse me. One of my spiritual gifts is teaching.

This passage is an excellent depiction of a pastor's wife or anyone's wife. I hear you Lord. A First Lady should be a woman of noble character. You know, I wish I could say I was the perfect virtuous woman. Thankfully, however, because of the Holy Spirit's guidance, I am a work in progress.

Love

In I Corinthians 13:4 – 8a, God defines what love is and what love is not. Let's focus on verses 7 and 8a. As a pastor's wife, I have learned emphatically that love ALWAYS protects, ALWAYS trusts, ALWAYS hopes, and ALWAYS perseveres. First Lady, you know the pastor better than anyone else in the church. God has entrusted you with the major responsibility of glorifying Him mightily by charging you with the ALWAYS love principle. Even when the enemy or you yourself don't feel like ALWAYS, loving as God commands and defines, brings honor to God and blesses you, your husband, the body of believers you serve and the unbelievers you will reach. In verse 8a, we see that love never fails.

Submission

Wives, submit to your husband as to the Lord (Ephesians 5:22). Yes, as his wife, you are commanded to submit to him. The Lord had to command it because He knew we would not do it on our own. Remember Eve. Submission is not bondage or inferiority. Submission is the ultimate case of freedom. First Ladies, who submit to their husbands, demonstrate the intended relationship between Christ and the church (Ephesians 5:22-24, 33b). Simply think of your submission to your husband as submission to God. In doing so, you will experience great blessings and thus full life. Submission takes the major responsibility off of you. As we are to submit to Christ in everything, so too are we to submit to our husbands in everything (Ephesians 5:24). Rebellion in this area hurts the body of believers. But you say, WAIT . . . I know the real pastor! How can I follow him always? Trust God and The God in the man.

Intimacy

One area the enemy loves to disturb in regard to God's chosen man is the intimacy between a man and his wife. Ladies, don't let the devil win this disturbance. Don't deprive him (I Corinthians 7:1-5). You have the upper hand in this matter. Please your man so that you may help him resist temptation. When I say please him, I mean be passionate and creative in the bedroom. Be affectionate. Be spontaneous. Write him love letters. Let him know that he is all the man you need. Let him know that you long for him. Compliment him more than anyone else. I hope this does not seem too racy or extreme. I prayed for God to increase my sexual appetite so that I might satisfy and bring my husband pleasure more frequently. Don't you know that prayer changes things.

Hopefully, you have not experienced this yet, but the anointing on your husband is magnetic. There may be that one woman who receives his counsel and pastoral attention that will want to show your husband her appreciation. Obviously, we know this is the enemy. As his first lady, you like no one else can have his back in this dilemma. Don't be jealous. Recognize the enemy. This cannot be ignored. Don't try to fight this battle alone. Remember God's Kingdom. He will protect His work. Pray and seek God. Obey God's guidance in the dealing with the matter; that is, follow the battle plan He gives you. God, who is faithful, will fight your battle. I can truly testify this to be true.

Support

As the pastor's wife and his first lady, you are to be his strongest supporter and encourager (Hebrews 10:25). What God has called the pastor to; He has also called the first lady to as his helper. Your presence is a strong indicator of support. When no one else shows up, you do. When no one else supports him, you do. When no one else believes in him as God's sent man, you do. Let him know that he has your backing 100%.

Communication

Communication is another major area the enemy attacks in marriage. The Pastor and First Lady should always communicate openly and without condemnation. One of the strongest points of my marriage has been communication. The books of Proverbs and James have much to teach us about the tongue. Govern your communication as such. Watch the attitude and mood swings when communicating. You know yourself. Men pick upon pitch and tone. In Proverbs 15:1 it says: "A gentle answer turns away wrath, but a harsh word stirs up anger." Knowing and applying this verse revolutionized my communication with my baby, oops, with my husband. We can help the way we talk. You say but what about . . . - but nothing. Obey God's Word and watch Him work.

His Children's Moma

Love all of your children. Train them. Teach them. Nurture them. Guide them. Prepare them to serve in ministry. Remember you are your husband's helper. Help him raise your children to have a firm start and foundation in life (Proverbs 22:6).

His Help

God has revealed to me with certainty that he prepared me especially for my husband to be his best friend, the loving mother of his children, his lover, his partner in life and his partner in ministry.

A Believer and a True Disciple

Are you saved?

A First Lady must be saved. Believe me there is no way a woman can walk in this role without being saved. Jesus must be the Lord and Savior of her life (Romans 10:9,10). Make sure Christ is the center of your life. As a First Lady, Jesus has shown that I must deny myself, take up my cross daily and follow Him. My name is Tracy. Tracy cannot be the center of my life. My husband's name is Dwayne. Dwayne cannot be the center of my life. In other words, he can't be my number one priority. Admittedly, I did have him in the spot at one time in my life. Believe me when I say God corrected that. The children cannot be the center of my life either. No person, place, thing, or position should be our top priority. In fact, Christ is in a category all by Himself. He should be The Priority. Everything else will fall in place.

True Discipleship

My relationship with God because of Jesus through the Holy Spirit is essential to my endurance and perseverance as I serve in ministry as the First Lady. As a born again believer, I have learned to be a true disciple of Christ. This is a must for a First Lady. Why? She serves the man of God like no one else does or is supposed to anyway, and she serves the body of believers God has blessed her husband to shepherd.

There are essentials to being a true disciple. Be filled with the Holy Spirit. The Holy Spirit resides within the believer. Listen to Him and follow His guidance. Depend on Him. It is through the Holy Spirit that we are able to love God and others and obey and bear lasting fruit.

Spend quiet time with God daily. Make a daily appointment with God and keep it (John 15:5). You can do nothing without him.

Live in the Word. How? Read It. Study It. Meditate on It. Listen to It. Memorize It. The Word of God is your spiritual nourishment. Holding to the Word of God sets you free (John 8:31-32). Be wise in the Word so that your life and counsel will serve to strengthen the Kingdom of God.

Pray in faith continually. Be a mighty prayer warrior.

First Ladies, pray! Nurture your fellow sisters and brothers in Christ. As First Lady, you are a big sista' in Christ. Share your life with those you serve. Love them like family. Loving them shows that you are a disciple of Jesus Christ (John 13:34-35).

Witness to the world. Share Christ with unbelievers. We are to bear much fruit; that is, new believers (John 15:8, Matthew 28:18-20).

Along with the pastor, the first lady, like Christ, must be willing to lay down her life for those she serves. Believe me when I say. I have learned that it is not about me individually but is about God and His chosen people. I know that First Ladies, who are true disciples of Christ, all over the world will agree with me when I say we are laying down our lives, denying ourselves, taking up our cross (which is ministry), and following Him. And this is not for our glory, but for the Glory of God.

A Servant-Leader

I have discovered that some people watch me, whether I like it or not. I try to ignore this fact and even pretend like it is not happening, but neither works. God has shown me that being the first lady or the pastor's wife is not for display. A first lady is a servant-leader. When people watch or let's say observe you, they are looking to see if you are going to really represent Christ. As a servant-leader chosen by God, I have learned that leadership is not a bad word when coupled with service. Servant-leadership is being an empty vessel available to be used by God. Whatever God pours into me is what I am to pour out. Then I will glorify Him because I am worshipping with my life. You see, a servant-leader knows that they are not the real leader – God is. Knowing this gives them a spirit of humility that takes on the same attitude of Christ – "nevertheless, not my will but your will be done." As a servant-leader, a first lady along with her husband, the pastor, is to surrender all for the sake of Christ.

What about me? – Soap Box Denied

I have not always known my purpose. I asked God, 'what about me? What do you want me to do?' I asked and He answered. The soapbox I desired was denied (Romans 12:1-2, Luke 9:23). He said I love you, but it is not about you. I said okay. He said you are a real woman with a real purpose (Colossians 1:16, Romans 11:36, Proverbs 16:4)). He said worship me with your life. I said I will. He said I made and shaped you especially for your husband, the pastor. I said is that all! He said proclaim My Word. I said yes to His will. Now, I am still asking how, and He reveals how daily and even now. One way I know I can proclaim it is through being a godly wife (a good mother), a true disciple, and a servant-leader before His people.

What I Have Realized

Being the First Lady for a body of believers is not glamorous despite perception. It is, however, self-sacrificing and husband sacrificing. All of my husband's time is not my time. Don't get me wrong. I do aid my husband by alerting him to those who want to monopolize his time or to those who want too much attention. After all, he does have a whole flock he serves.

Being the First Lady is lonely at times. Oftentimes there is no one to talk to about what goes on at home. You know what I mean, Ladies. Our households are no different from anyone else's. We are confronted with problems and difficulties too – with children, with finances, with our husbands, with extended family, with jobs, with coworkers, and so on and so on. It is hard for others to accept that your life is not perfect. They are trying to follow your lead. What do I do in such circumstances: I can only turn to God. He then assures me that He is with me all the way. In my mind and spirit, I seek to build the Kingdom not tear it down by temporary happenings in my personal life.

Earlier I said something about some first ladies seeming to be phony at times based on my observations. Now perhaps I know why. They may have the same mind as me – desiring not to misrepresent God, rather desiring above all else that God be glorified further advancing the Kingdom. So, sometimes she must wear masks for the sake of magnifying God in the presence of His people.

I have realized that I am not in control at all. I really think this a weakness of most, especially women. God is in full control! He is indeed sovereign.

Serving and caring for God's people is rewarding. Experiencing God as He works in the lives of others miraculously by changing hearts, relationships, and circumstances is unmatched by anything I could ever hope to experience.

I am now more aware of when the enemy is attacking. I try not to panic. God has clearly instructed us in His Word to Trust Him fully. His instructions are simple: Trust God fully! Obey God! Love all, which includes your enemies! Forgive and forget – Love is a function of forgiveness! Let Go and Let God – stop trying to be in control and submit to God's sovereignty.

First Lady – What a Call and Responsibility

Okay, Okay! I can humbly accept being called First Lady. No, I don't want to be on a pedestal. I am still not phony. I will be approachable because God tells me to fellowship with believers and witness to the world. I know who I am in Christ. Thank you, God for your definition. Thank you for using me despite me. Being called First Lady is a call and responsibility that signifies that we have been chosen by God to reflect His glory as we serve God, our husbands, our families, and God's people.

CONCLUSION

ach of these women has shared nine different perspectives as a First Lady. Remember, their perspective may not be your perspective, their issues may not be your issues but, we serve a God that whatever your perspective or issues are, He is able to handle your situation.

This book was written out of our hearts to encourage you to fight for your rightful place in the kingdom of God. We will no longer run from our problems but we will face them knowing God has gone ahead of us to fight on our behalf.

My prayer is that in your reading of this book, God

has confirmed your purpose and strengthened you to lead His people in whatever role you serve in. I would hope that you now share your heart and be a blessing to each person whom God allows to cross your path.

From this day forward, let "From the Hearts of First Ladies" help you move beyond the pain of your past, live each moment for God and impart into the lives of others that they may know what it means to have a tomorrow.

I thank God for you and I am honored that He used me and these awesome First Ladies to share our hearts.

Finally, to the First Ladies who shared their hearts and made this book a possibility, I love you all dearly. I pray God's anointing will forever be upon you and that you experience great joy knowing you made an impact in the many lives who will receive a blessing from this book.

I love you always!

ABOUT THE AUTHOR

Debbie Elaine Hawkins

Debbie Elaine Hawkins co-labors in ministry with her husband, Bishop Gary Hawkins, Sr., the Founding Pastor of Voices of Faith Ministries in Stone Mountain and Conyers, Georgia. She is Founder of Women with Voices (a women's ministry) to strengthen women with the word of God. She is, also, the Founder & CEO of (DHM) **Debbie E. Hawkins Ministries** an entity given to her by God to transform the lifestyles of individuals by ministering and demonstrating through God's Word. Debbie and her husband, Gary, live in Loganville, Georgia with their four children, Elaina, Ashley, Gary Jr. and Kalen.

ORDER FORM

Order by phone, fax, mail, or online.

Debbie Hawkins Ministries

P.O. Box 871172
Stone Mountain, Georgia 30087
Phone: 770.498.5850   Fax: 770.498.1566
Email: vof@voicesfaith.org   Website: www.voicesfaith.org

QTY	ITEM	EACH	TOTAL
_____	From the Hearts of First Ladies	$15.95	_____
_____	What Every First Lady Should Know	$14.95	_____
_____	Faith Journal	$10.00	_____
_____	There Is A Word Daily Devotional	**Coming Soon**	

BOOKS AUTHORED BY: BISHOP GARY HAWKINS SR.

_____	What Every Pastor Should Know	$15.95	_____
_____	Marketing Your Church for Growth	$12.95	_____
_____	Marketing for Next Level Ministry	$15.95	_____
_____	8 Steps to Prosperity - Book	$15.95	_____
_____	God's Best For Your Life	$15.95	_____
_____	Fighting for Your Destiny	$13.95	_____
_____	**SUBTOTAL**		_____
_____	Postage and Handling (Call for Shipping Charges)		_____
_____	**TOTAL**		_____

NAME: _____ DATE: _____

ADDRESS: _____ APT./UNIT: _____

CITY: _____ STATE: _____ ZIP: _____

PAYMENT METHOD: ❏ VISA ❏ MC ❏ AMEX ❏ DISCOVER ❏ CHECK

CREDIT CARD # _____ EXP.: _____

SIGNATURE: _____